About the Author

The author has studied psychology, history, archaeology, and engineering for over two decades. This has led him to the doorsteps of religion, philosophy, spirituality, and metaphysics in pursuing the truth about the human condition. The idea for this book came in 2008 after he spent forty days and nights in the Tunisian part of the Sahara Desert contemplating and reading. His childhood dream was to know all secrets in the universe, and he intends to die curious.

WHERE
The Metaphysics of Matter

Dennis Cobélean

WHERE
The Metaphysics of Matter

Vanguard Press

VANGUARD PAPERBACK

© Copyright 2024
Dennis Cobélean

A CIP catalogue record for this title is
available from the British Library.

ISBN 978 1 83794 148 3

*Vanguard Press is an imprint of
Pegasus Elliot Mackenzie Publishers Ltd.*
www.pegasuspublishers.com

First Published in 2024

**Vanguard Press
Sheraton House Castle Park
Cambridge England**

Printed & Bound in Great Britain

For my wife, Malin: Thank you for breaking my pattern.

Those who have inspired me to seek knowledge and author this book. Jiddu Krishnamurti, David Bohm, Terence and Dennis Mckenna, Graham Hancock, Kreia, China Miéville, Siddhartha Gautama, Jesus, The Nag Hamidi, Lao Tzu, Chuang tzu, Plotinus, Paul Coelho, Esther Hicks, Olaf Stapledon, Douglas Adams, Neil Gaiman, Carl Jung, Ngusi wa Thiongo, Iching, Dögen, Mark Passio, Viktor Schauberger, Jason Gregory, The Kybalion, David R Hawkins, Firefly Taro, White Feather Taro, Roseology and endlessly more. BLUME, thanks for the music. Remember, my path is my path. What I draw knowledge from is what I draw knowledge from. You cannot stop searching for truth. Find your path and find your teachers.

Whispering in your ears, whispering in your ears something relevant but hard to understand. You go crazy when you learn. You go so crazy when you learn. You go crazy when you learn to understand.

Johan Jonason

THE STUDY OF 10 000 THINGS

This book will only make sense to those who have already understood its meaning, repeating what is already felt and known. Thus, this book is entirely pointless and is a recollection of what is known.

In the study of 10 000 things, we will closely examine matter, what it is, and how it is essential for our purpose. The purpose of this book is at first unclear or obscure from our minds and sight because of the nature of our goal, which is hard to grasp and even harder to realise. In the journey you and I are embarking on, few have seen, and even fewer have walked it.

Our STUDY OF 10 000 THINGS will lead us to the *study of two things*, leading to our goal, the *study of one thing*. This thing is not a thing and has never been a thing, but by studying it, we will reach our destination. This *nothing* I am referring to cannot be known by the mind or explained by words. It must be felt, infused, remembered by the soul, and our hearts must agree to impart the wisdom of this *nothing*, or we will not get there, which is nowhere but blossoms out to everywhere.

I wish us both good luck and safe travels. May we reach where we need to be, not where we want to be.

Freedom is a road seldom travelled by the multitude but an inherent birthright.

Yours in Love, Understanding, and Gratitude.

Dennis Cobélean

2021-02-17

Chapter 1

What is matter, what is it made of, and how is it constituted? If we are to believe the scientists, matter is a non-living, potential energy that one can hold or store, which has mass and volume, atoms, and electrons. This thinking leads us to a dead end regarding the living entities of the universe. No dead thing can give life to something living. I am almost sure there is not, nor has there ever been, a genuinely dead thing in the universe, devoid of movement and vibration. A dead thing would be a horrific thing to see. Our very being would be aghast in disbelief. We would revolt against its very existence as an affront to life and all that we know, so no, matter is not a dead thing.

All physical things are made of atoms, electrons, and even smaller particles. All these particles move and vibrate, creating a connection, a miniature solar system, and energy or power is generated between them. Matter is solid or frozen energy. As the atoms gather, the electrons spinning around each atom join and share atoms with each other. The pathways the electrons create become solid, and only the outermost electrons rotate more freely, but all the electrons are still present. When we heat a solid piece of matter, the electrons and atoms start to vibrate faster, and the pathways start to dissolve, breaking the matter into particles. A process called combustion, and heat energy is released.

I have deliberately not used the word 'force' because that implies that one or more particles are forcing the others to stay in place. Force means intent, sometimes malicious, to hold or bind another particle or entity in bondage for some beneficial activity or event. So, if this were true, that would mean that when it comes to matter, slavery is the norm. That all matter, all material things, are working under the principle of slavery in the whole universe. This, in turn, means that slavery would be a natural phenomenon and all things would be bound to it, then God would be the ultimate slave owner, and free will would never be a thought in our hearts and minds.

The particles are moving, dancing around each other because they choose to cooperate. They decided to bind themselves to each other in mutually beneficial respect for each other and love; all parts receive what they need in this relationship, and this is how all-natural relationships work in the universe. Matter is mostly empty space, a cluster of electrons, protons, and neutrons, so what holds a substance together, and how is it formed? The energy generated in an atom holds it together, and the constant generating of energy at the same levels makes it stable. Hydrogen is the atom that all other atoms are formed from. I will come back to this later. The mass of electrons, protons, and neutrons is less in higher dimensions and more in lower dimensions.

In higher dimensions, the energy generated is greater in and by atoms because of less inertia, so the mass is less, and the particle in an atom vibrates faster, generating more energy in the atom. In the highest dimension, everything is pure energy and no mass. The energy levels are low in the lowest dimension, but the mass is pervasive. Atoms form when three particles cooperate with mutual love and harmony to create a new atom or substance. The universe works from the principle of collaboration, love, and unity to benefit the whole. Every part benefits all other parts. That is why the universe is self-generating and can sustain all conscious beings. Life creates life.

What is so essential with matter is that we and the world around us are made of these base materials. For thousands of years, spiritual leaders have told us to do away with material things, not give them meaning and importance or give them up altogether. This is contradictory. Why is it bad for us if all matter is life, consciousness, and ultimate pure energy? Focusing on the matter, not the energy part, we miss the point with our experience on this plane. We will assign importance to things with little energy and discard energy-rich things, with high potential energy.

By choosing energy-deficient objects to focus on or give importance to, we will not get energised or rejuvenated by them. Instead, we will feel tired, drained, hollow, and poor, so we will hunt for more of the same in the false belief that more will energise us. One must see the truth about the things we give value to investigate them. Do they really hold high energy or potential energy? If not, they will make you feel lacking and poor and, in fact, steal your energy. Hydrogen has the highest potential energy content of all matter. This leads us to Einstein's equation $E=mC^2$. This equation proves that all matter is energy or light in arrested form or frozen.

Chapter 2

Humans attach great value to different metals or gems, not realising that the lower or baser materials are the building blocks of the higher ones. Lower materials transform and develop according to the natural laws of the universe. All things and materials strive to evolve to raise their energy levels. All things seek to reach higher dimensions to shed matter and become pure energy. When a pivotal point is reached, the universe will retreat into itself and begin anew. Sentient beings aim to transform their own matter into more fluid living energy, trailblazing for others, indicating that it is possible. This notion is an old one. All the alchemists of old held this belief, and it was their focal point in their practice of alchemy to transform lead into gold.

Contrary to popular belief, monetary gains were not their aim; instead, they aimed for a higher and deeper price, but still so intrinsically natural to all sentient beings that it is mind-blowing. Many of the old alchemists failed in their quest. The reasons for this are as many as those who tried. I think the main reason would be that their will and ego were in the way, making it impossible to achieve this goal. As I said earlier, nothing can force another thing to become something it does not want to become or is not ready to evolve into. Water, Earth, Air, and Fire, the four elements that make up our world, represent the different aspects of matter. Of these four elements, Fire is not a substance.

Scientists would call it a chemical reaction or a thermal event, but what is it? If we play with these elements, then Air reacts with Earth to create Fire, but Water puts the Fire out. Although there is Air and hydrogen in Water, which is highly flammable, so what is going on? Fire or heat cannot ignite Water. When hydrogen reacts with oxygen (Air), it creates Water. Can one substance react with another substance that will produce the first substance? Can you be the mother and child to yourself. Fire is the medium through which substances transform. It is a transformative agent that allows a substance to shed the old and transform into something new with less matter and more energy or potential energy. Pressure with heat is Fire without oxygen. A fire or explosion will occur if enough oxygen is introduced to the pressure point.

As the phoenix bird renews after burning, the forest fire renews the forest shedding old or dead material to make room for new. Fire is rapid oxygen consumption producing heat, so our next question is, what is heat? I will briefly touch upon this subject so that we can move forward. A straightforward way of describing heat and cold is that atoms move fast or slow. Heat is fast-moving atoms, and cold is slow-moving atoms, but is it this simple? The universe is a cold place, $3°$ Celsius above zero or absolute freezing point, where atoms cannot move. If space had been any colder, nothing would move, so nothing would form. Because of gravitational forces, objects can pull and attract objects to them so that clouds of hydrogen and helium can create stars, elements, and planets.

This minuscule difference in temperature of only 3 degrees is pivotal for movement but slow enough so that not too much heat is generated because if it were, we would be in trouble. When atoms bump into each other, they heat up and move faster. If the universe had been warmer, it would have taken longer for the gravitational forces to attract matter. The atoms would move too fast to be attracted, and form gas clouds, stars, and planets. The fast-moving atoms would slam into each other under gravitational forces and generate heat, maybe enough heat to cause explosions in a stage that would hinder or completely arrest the development of gas clouds, stars, etc.

If the universe had been colder, nothing would form due to no movement, and if the universe had been warmer, nothing would form due to fast movement and heat. Cold is unmoving, death, but also the birth of new life. Heat is moving, life, but also the beginning of death. Both cold and heat burns. They are the opposite of each other but essentially the same. In this book, the element Fire is a medium that transforms matter, but it is not matter.

Chapter 3

We must make matter our friend and understand that it is a mutual co-creating component that is a part of us. If one could truly feel and make a reality of that knowledge in oneself. You would never go hungry or sick again. You could give the body exactly what it needs to function optimally in every second of your life. Your body is only a vessel for the consciousness that holds this truth, and as long as you are reading this book, talk to the body and listen to it and try to be one with it. Notice how things start to change around you, how your body will harmonise with your loving, grateful conscious thinking.

Matter is less solid than it appears to be. We know this already, but only on an intellectual level. This thinking makes matter more solid than it is. If we could truly feel that matter and our sense of perception were as flexible as our consciousness, matter would not appear to be so solid.

In our everyday life, most of us move our bodies around how we choose to. This action of moving the body seems natural to most of us. It is done with little energy output, but what are we doing when we move around? When we move from here to there, we guide our body with our intention, where to go and what to do. Most of us would say that this is easy to do, but other activities requiring the mind are harder to do. This act of moving your body is quite astonishing since you are intentionally altering the body's functions to achieve your goal, more blood, and oxygen to some necessary part with your mind alone.

This 'simple' act of moving around signifies that we can influence matter with our minds to aid us in life. A mutually beneficial relationship where life serves life. We believe that our body is separate from other matter, and since my body is a separate object, all objects are separate. This is not true, and a simple thought experiment can shed some light on this. Let us say you could see everything on an atomic level using a pair of glasses. First, you see a car, a bird, and a person. In between them, there is Air. You put the glasses on and now see the same thing but on an atomic level. You would see clusters or clouds of atoms that moved around. We can assign a colour to each group of atoms since each atom vibrates at different speeds sending out different wavelengths of light. You would see different colour clusters that moved around in empty space.

If the cluster were richer or darker in its colours, that would represent a higher concentration of those atoms, but they would be a mix of many colours since each object has a multitude of different atoms. Let us say that the bird is a mix of red, blue, and green when it lands on the car. The car is a mix of green, yellow, and orange. How would this event appear to you? A small colourful cloud attaches itself to a bigger, colourful cloud, and they seem to join. Being indistinguishable from each other, becoming one, not two separate objects or clouds. For example, the iron atoms in the bird would not be distinguishable from the iron atoms in the car, and you would not be able to see which belonged to whom, and oxygen atoms in the bird and the car would all intermingle with each other in the same way.

On the atomic level, all solids would look temporarily conjoined. Atoms would change places with each other, move around, and jump. You would not be able to distinguish one object from the next. What does this mean, that all matter is less solid and unchangeable than we think? The atom in an object moves or changes according to its intentions and in cooperation with other atoms. To expand and benefit each other, the larger cluster of atoms (the object) and the universe. So how can we change matter and transform one object into the next? All matter is ready to transform. It wants to evolve into something new. This inherent 'will' to change can be influenced so the object makes that leap. Still, our will must be noncoercive *'Wuwei'*, and we cannot expect a benefit or take advantage of this transformation but see it as the goal for the transformation.

To be and live noncoercive can be perceived is hard, surrendering one's will and power to the universe. What will we get in return? To expect a return will give us nothing. Only non-expectation will yield us all that we need and strength. Matter wants to change to be of service. It wants to be a link in a chain that is evolving the universe.

Chapter 4

In our dreams or when we fantasise, we create objects or entities for their beauty or utility. It is like climbing a mountain only for its view. This act of creation is critical to explore to train our intentions before we transform an object. You have probably heard that observing a system or object transforms it. This is a common fact in the world of science. By observing a system, the observer changes the system. This implies one of three things. The system changes by itself because someone observes it, which implies consciousness. Or the observer influences, or forces the system to change, or the last option is that it is a co-creation where both parties recognise each other's intentions and collaborate to realise the best outcome. And as a result, both parties change and evolve.

Why do both parties evolve? If A can change, see, or move B, then B can do the same to A and will. Force can be used, but that would mean that forced will, and energy is introduced to the system. So that a specific outcome occurs that is not a natural outcome. As I have said earlier, force can be a malicious intention to bring about a favoured result regardless of what the other party or parties think or want for themselves. Disregarding the natural, spontaneous of serendipitous events of meetings or occurrences. You can train yourself to be noncoercive in your behaviour, thinking, and doing. This might lead you to a place where being peaceful within you is natural. When that state of mind is reached, to influence or cooperate, co-create with matter will be done consciously with love, respect, and mutual benefit and at the right time. To train yourself in noncoercive thinking and acting, you can use daydreaming, fantasising, and imagining yourself creating all things you desire, but only for their beauty or utility.

The things you create can serve and please others just by existing in your mind's eye. By training your mind to make things for others for the creation itself, you are helping yourself not to have expectations. Only create so that others may enjoy what you have created. This regards your thoughts, speech, and actions as well. All of it is creating, and when others enjoy your creation, you enjoy creating and understand that you are an important part of creation. It means to be in service to others and the universe making it more beautiful, fuller of life. Making more choices with your love for what you have created. For others and the universe, this is the state of true bliss. You must relinquish the 'good' feeling when you give something away, and the receiver appreciates the gift. Only focus on the love of creating, enhancing love and beauty in the universe. Train yourself to let go of all ego-boosting, all self-appreciating, and focus only on the bliss of creating. Focus on creating and the creation around you, people, animals, trees, rocks, and the outline of a coastline.

Natural things have an inner beauty that, even if it rots or crumbles, that inner beauty still shines forth. Things that we make might be beautiful but still lack something. Often the things we find beautiful are made of 'natural' materials and handmade. We as a people like paintings and sculptures where the creator's intention shines through. We value the nonphysical part of the object most. This includes people and especially *you*. When other humans perform acts that we are awed about, martial arts, gymnastics, football, or dancing, it is the movement with the intention that we are in awe of, not the body. Beauty is always the nonphysical part of the physical object or performance. There is beauty in an axe for its utility and practicality, not just in its design.

When an expert in axe handling swings the axe, the combination of handling, utility, performance, and design comes into play. The metaphysical and the material join to display an act full of beauty, and we are in awe. A beautiful dancer performs a perfect dance. Someone wields an axe, hammer, football, or her body. So that the actor can perfectly display the love of the utility and design of the physical object, heaven is spiritual but also practical. The purpose of understanding what matter is, is to become a mutual co-creator in our own time and this physical realm. We must learn to see and feel that we are a part of all matter and that our physical body has no beginning or end. We extend to all corners of this universe.

When you evolve, the universe evolves, and when the universe evolves, you do too. When we are conscious of our true physical form and how all matter is connected, then natural order and love are enhanced in the universe. Unconsciousness leads to disorder, leading to fear. Order and chaos are only based on what the conscious mind can perceive. What looks like chaos to the unconscious mind is a specific order to the conscious mind. On the scale of humans, when it comes to chaos, it is an aspect of the unconscious, fearful mind that wants to control or at least have a basic understanding of what is happening. The conscious mind does not see chaos but a perfect system that has a purpose and a direction. The conscious, loving mind knows that disorder only exists in the fearful mind.

Chapter 5

To be a co-creator, one must overcome the feeling and programming that our bodies are separate from other matter in the universe. We must also become loving and in love with creating. By letting go of preconceived ideas and programming, we can start to feel and understand that all matter is a part of us. This true understanding will eventually lead us closer to our goal. By being in love with creating, we must also be in love with matter and ourselves. This self-love is a prerequisite to being a creator. By loving yourself, and your body, you love matter, and thus the creation and creating. The opposite of creating is destruction. Destruction does not exist in the sense we think and use the word.

To destroy is to pull down a house, tree, statue, or the world that one inhabits, in such a way it cannot be rebuilt but must be replaced. Since matter is energy, so what we refer to when we say destruction, is the destruction of matter, not energy, since it cannot be destroyed. Material objects can be destroyed, pulled down, or picked apart so they cannot be rebuilt, causing irreversible damage to an object. In this regard, destruction exists on a material level but not on an energy level. When something gets destroyed, we mean or imply that an agent acted on the object with force to destroy it. This implies that the destruction was done before the natural death and decomposition of the object.

Destruction is an action performed by an actor with intent or a series of events to bring about the object's destruction. In a harmonious natural system, the destruction of anything might not occur. The causes for an object's destruction are many but often hidden from our sight, especially in nature. Hurricanes might look natural to us, but are they? This is not an easy question to answer, and I will not try, but please ponder this question. Death and decomposition of an object are natural if left to its own accord. Destruction is not natural or timely. It pre-empts the time of death and jump-starts decomposition. The closest we come to destruction is when we split the atom. This destruction of the nucleus, ripping apart the bonds by force, is done with intention.

Not even this event of splitting the atom destroys matter. Matter is not matter but energy, and energy cannot be destroyed. The reason for us being on this plane with matter is to create. Creating is what we humans do, and we have always done it but on a superficial level. We create with our hands to transform matter into objects. Objects that are created by our fantasy, books, films, paintings, and music are more durable because they are worlds and universes, entities that entice us to dream. The female and male bodies are remarkably similar, even if we cover them with clothes. It is easy to recognise one from the other, even from afar. Why is this? Females sometimes have a body that looks male and vice versa, but still, we can often see or know the difference.

Dead bodies of males and females are almost indistinguishable from each other, so what happened? When consciousness disappears from the body, the matter that remains is just matter. This implies that we recognise the consciousness or the energy of that consciousness as life. Matter is energy, which we can influence to create or change matter or objects. By using a method like 'letting go', 'chi gong', or any other method, we can easily change and heal the matter in our body, but what of other objects? Changing and influencing objects and matter outside of the body is as easy as changing the matter in the body. The difficulty is recognising that 'foreign' matter is not separate or foreign but an extension or a part of you. There is one caveat though: trying to influence another being's matter is not recommended, we once again cross paths with force, power, and free will. You should not under any circumstances force your will on another sentient being. It must be done with love, understanding, mutual respect, and benefit.

Chapter 6

There is a difference between being alive and living. As I said in the beginning, all matter is living, but that does not mean all matter is alive. A lump of coal or iron is living, but a tree is alive. All things that feed are alive, and those who do not feed are living. The consciousness expresses itself in a more complex way in an alive entity than in a living object because of the entanglement in matter. This creates a survival instinct and a will to evolve and transcend the entity's current form to a higher form. Living objects have a consciousness that is more in tune with the laws and God's plan. It is more set in its form. But the willingness to evolve is high. Matter that is alive is more flexible in its form, but the willingness to evolve is lower. Consciousness has a purpose that drives matter into a predetermined form. Living objects are open or want to change into a higher order object; if a consciousness influences the object, it will happily cooperate to change.

On the other hand, an alive entity will not be influenced to that degree since it has its own purpose and timetable to follow. One can be part of another entity's evolution if it cooperates willingly for mutual benefit. This must be on the entity's timetable. Then, one can help or guide it to its new form. The first object one should influence is one's body, to heal it or change things about it that would be for the better. Regrow hair, improve eyesight, and so on. This can be done. The smaller or more 'believable' the improvements are, the easier they are to realise. Start small and believe that you can do it and allow time to pass so that the transformation of your belief can manifest in your body. One can begin influencing other objects by realising the power of one's consciousness to affect matter. Practice makes confidence.

Solid matter has the lowest energy content, and it is only possible to influence an object if you hold more energy than that object. For instance, a three-volt battery cannot turn the starter motor in a car. You need a car battery to do that. The same goes for living objects and consciousness. A 'weaker', scared, conflicted, or confused mind can easily be influenced to agree to actions or beliefs that are wrong and non-moral by a focused consciousness. Since the conscious mind has a high energy level, that energy can be amplified by other minds with the same energy frequency.

This is how non-moral beliefs and actions become the norm in societies. A high-energy system starts to ignite lower-energy systems. The lower join with the higher and increase the higher to greater levels making it easier to ignite lower-energy systems. Until the higher, acting energy system becomes an unstoppable force. This is only possible when a society has a lot of fear, confusion, or conflicts within itself, acting on the minds of all the participants in that society. Scared and/or confused minds do not act or listen to their own heart or consciousness. Making them open to influence or submission to that belief or action one propagates. Today the 'best' or most effective way to create fear, confusion, and conflicts is to disturb or restrict the flow of money. When that happens, most minds go apeshit, and a malicious mind can and, will influence that society to agree on its beliefs and actions.

This is, however, not how benevolent minds work, minds that are synchronised with their consciousness and heart. Those minds want to raise the energy levels in a system because they want that system to evolve, but of its own volition and time frame. It is like raising a child. Most of us do not try to rush the child's evolution, trying to make her run before she can crawl. This philosophy does not directly influence and inspire change or revolution, but only indirectly. It influences the mind that listens to the philosophy to question its thoughts and actions. It inspires the listener to examine the connection between the heart, consciousness, mind and its thoughts. And if, and only if the listener can "see" his/her disharmony they can choose to evolve. That free mind tries to influence and inspire others to do the same.

This type of evolution is from the heart, consciousness, and not the mind. It is a slow evolution but solid if it can run its course to fruition. This is why benevolent philosophies seldom prevail in society. They are too slow. In a world that spins faster and faster, few take the time to listen to them. Can we speed up this process or make more people listen? The answer to that question will be revealed in book three, *WHY - The study of One Thing*. Remember, we must learn to crawl before we fly. All matter wants to evolve into an object with higher energy content, by its own volition. Or with the aid or influence of a high-energy object or person. This is the reason people go to gurus and look for spiritual leaders so that they can help or guide us to raise our energy levels.

Some places or people can help us to achieve this. Unfortunately, many return to their default setting when they are away from the person or place. We want to evolve our matter, so it contains more energy. One must reach the tipping point when trying to influence an object or person, where the new energy level in the object is self-generating and sustainable. Beginners often have problems with this decisive step because it confirms that we are powerful creators. This confirmation is hard to accept because it means we have lived in denial of our true power, which saddens us immensely.

How do we reach this tipping point? The simple answer is that one must know in one's heart that it is possible to change the object truly and completely. To genuinely believe, you must know that with every fibre of your being. All doubt must be eradicated from your heart. Your confidence in your creative, healing power must be self-evident, as when you move your arm, open an eye, or take a step. Move your mind into the field of consciousness, that higher state of being where your heart and soul are, where all uncertainty disappears. Matter wants to evolve, the only thing hindering evolution is doubt, especially when it comes to sentient beings. You can change an object and its composition, but only within its limits which is the object's mass. This applies to all objects, internal or external.

Chapter 7

I did not expect to write about how to reach the stage where you can begin to influence or change your body or objects, but I realise that I must. We must learn to let go of negative feelings and emotions, all the limiting beliefs we sustain to validate our person and existence. You are neither this nor that. You are the true you, the void manifest in the flesh, all possibilities all creating consciousness in a body. When we think of limiting beliefs, we usually think of negative or detrimental thoughts about the world or ourselves. Even positive thinking is limiting since you make borders of it in your mind. For instance, if you believe you are a good singer and you need to sing as you have never sung before, is that possible? Or you have a great imagination. Can you be bad at imagining things? Can you unlearn what you have learnt or believe about yourself at will?

There are many methods to help you let go of notions, feelings, and beliefs. Shop around until you find one or more that works for you. The importance and the necessity of this are crucial for our quest to succeed in our life, not in life but in your life. We can clear a path ahead by disregarding negative and positive emotions, notions, and beliefs about ourselves. Our will and ego will no longer oversee our life; thus, we will be open to the nature of the universe. This will allow God to work through and for us to achieve the best outcome in every situation. Our ego masquerades itself as volition so that we, believe that we want or do not want to achieve something or another. The reason for this is that the ego is short-sighted and focuses on the survival of itself and the 'normal' mental state of its person.

The ego does not trust the universe, so it tries to assert itself in every situation. This causes the illusion of control to arise. This illusion is almost never complete, so feelings of fear, anxiety, and not reaching the heart of your life are always present: a hole in your heart that you can never fill. When we think I am not worthy, intelligent, beautiful, and so on, it is not the words that make us feel bad. It is the feeling of not being enough. Not being a part of the universe, but separated and broken, lonely. This feeling of separation is perceived as real. This makes us feel powerless, and the ego steps in to control the situation. The ego confirms the illusion of our separation from the universe and applies force to rectify the situation.

As Jung said, the ego is born and maintained by the inner world colliding with the outer world. This results in the belief that the ego is our friend helping and defending us. In reality, it is the opposite. The ego leads us further and further away from our true selves and the nature of the universe. The ego wants to isolate us from the 'hostile' universe to secure survival and influence over its person. For most people, it succeeds in this endeavour, and we become NPCs or Non-Playing Characters in the universe. Where your life and actions can be meaningless. When you stop obeying your ego, the power that created the universe is at your disposal. Only with power can we influence matter; true power is love because it will never do anything that goes against the laws of the universe.

In conclusion, one must surrender negative feelings and emotions to reconnect with one's true power. The same power that created the universe and we have access to it. We must trust in this power and know we have it because we are a part of this universe and everything in it. The work can begin now, as we are grounded and can act like a vessel for the universe's intention. Influencing matter in your body might be a big new capacity you are beginning to experience. The key is not to let your will or ego be in the way. You will soon find that influencing matter is relatively easy to do. It is easy when there is no resistance, and the purpose is to benefit the whole.

It becomes hard when you do it for a separate part or a purpose that only supports your ego. A mind that separates from the whole must use force to do things since it does not trust or believe in a benevolent universe. When we observe matter, we recognise certain properties. Are these properties all-encompassing and permanent for that substance? The human observer sees a piece of steel and pretty much knows its properties. Steel is hard, easy to heat, and so on, but is that accurate? Most observers bring their prejudice to the observation and transfer it to the object, solidifying the mind's illusion about the object. Let us say a being from the fifth dimension would observe the same piece of steel. Would this entity describe the same properties, or would it see something else?

By seeing all objects as they truly are, we can begin to understand the fundamentals of creation. On the atomic level, all objects look the same and have the same particles. I believe that when you manipulate matter in your body, you manipulate it at the atomic level. We know how to change the orbits of electrons and attract protons and neutrons. Some have built a Large Hadron Collider, but can we do it with our minds, affect the direction of electrons, protons or neutrons or move them all together. It seems easier to affect matter at the atomic level than to get someone to understand that they can learn to do it, which is ironic. The proton is positive, the electron is negative, and the neutron is neutral. This is the form, all matter is built in the universe (as far as we know), so let us look at these components.

The proton and electron have the same energy but opposite charges; the neutron and proton have the mass, and the electron is very light. The proton and neutron are the anchors in the atom, and as the electron spins around the nucleolus, energy is created. The neutron and proton stabilise the electron's orbit, speed, and energy level. The p & n attracts electrons, so if we could add a p & n to the nucleolus of an atom, it would attract another electron, and you would have a new type of atom.

Chapter 8

All things in the universe seek equilibrium. To reach this state of equilibrium, the universe will sacrifice everything and anything. This seems hard or abhorrent to some people, but if we look at it, it makes perfect sense. Equilibrium implies perfect balance and mutual benefit, and it is a natural law in the universe, so we must seek equilibrium and mutual benefit. This state is the prerequisite to our success. We must understand this, or we will not succeed in our endeavour. However, I must mention that this state is an unnatural natural state. All things strive to be in equilibrium within themselves and the universe, but it is at the beginning and the end that we reach it. Matter is neither gross nor evil nor binds you to the physical plane. It is just the material that the physical universe is made of.

Without matter, the universe would only be mind. The notion of the noble spirit falling or sinking into the evil, dirty matter insults the universe and God. I believe that this notion can make us blind to the possibility that matter gives us an understanding of ourselves and the universe. Matter is a vessel for the spirit, and one such material vessel is the 'Philosopher's stone'. Without this vessel, we cannot transform ourselves or reach our intended goal. This stone is extremely rare but can be found everywhere, and no words can describe it. We must reconcile with matter and see it for what it is, an ally in our life because it is only together that we can transform ourselves. Mutual benefit is the key.

Everything we see in the world is made up of matter. In this matter, there is energy. A landscape that is in harmony is also mutually beneficing all living things. The energy level in a harmonious landscape is enhanced beyond the combined energy levels of all living things. Things that are in balance and harmony create more energy than they use. When we look at the beautiful landscape, the matter may be beautiful. But it is the energy that flows harmoniously in the landscape and the living things that we perceive as beautiful. Therefore, we do not find small, wooded areas (parks) in the city as tranquil or relaxing as a forest. Its function, energy flow, is not working properly.

The same thing can be said about heavily organised gardens, they seem lifeless and boring to the mind and the eye. An object that loses its purpose loses energy and beauty. A pile of firewood is not as beautiful as the tree it came from. There is enough wealth and resources for all creatures. Nothing needs to go without or be lacking. By knowing and feeling that all matter is there to be of service to us, we are here not only to enjoy this service but to reciprocate it. Since in all matter, there is a consciousness that knows its intrinsic purpose. We have a purpose, but ours is more elusive due to human nature and the possibility that this nature grants us.

Creating tangible, intangible and even impossible things is not a fortunate accident. Matter and living beings that are less complex than us is slower and more resistant to evolution. It takes many thousands of years for them to reach the next level of evolution. Less complex matter or beings need time or a powerfully focused consciousness to direct the necessary energy needed to perform the transformation it is subjected to or wants. We live in this material world to learn how to create and transform material and immaterial objects in our reality. Expand life and the experience of this universe for ourselves and all living creatures in it. If this universe were only of pure energy, would evolution be needed? Could there be different types of energy fields in different stages of development, and how would these fields interact?

The different energy fields would intermingle and then merge into a uniform equilibrium field with a single energy content. There would be no need for any evolution in this field, or is the act of reaching equilibrium the evolution? Matter is energy, but energy is also energy. Can there be energy without matter? Is energy without matter potential energy or mental energy? Before our universe existed, was there any matter, which would imply that our universe sprung out of the corpse of an older universe? If this is not the case, there could not have been any matter when the first universe was created. When the first universe was created, there was only energy. After the 'big bang', some of that energy was calcified into matter, binding that energy or light into matter. If the first universe was created from a field of energy, and that field was in harmony, what made it explode?

Physical or mental objects in harmony and balance can change or evolve in three ways: firstly, external influence, secondly, inner clarity. The third way is when inner clarity and external influence coincide. Then the change or evolution will be more rapid, but this may only apply to conscious beings. If the change is brought on by external influence, something, or someone 'poked' our energy field. This made the energy field unstable, resulting in a chain reaction that created our universe. From where did this external thing come? But if the change was brought on by internal clarity, a want, need or will, to change, then our energy field had a consciousness that caused the chain reaction to create our universe.

Regardless of how we look at it, our universe could not have been created by chance of itself. Something or someone initiated the chain reaction that created the universe. This is how all things evolve, through either external influence or internal clarity. Or in those rare moments when both coincide, as above so below. This system of evolution is connected to time as well. External influence is the past. The combination of external and internal is the present, and internal clarity is the future. To change matter, we must influence the object, raise the energy level within the object, and when the object's energy is unbalanced, we give it a last push, and it will change and become anew.

Chapter 9

In this material world we live in, matter is in abundance, but it is the energy in matter that is important. We are, by default, powerful creators, and if we could learn how to dispel our mental fog. To remember what we are and activate our body and mind, we could rediscover our true and natural purpose. Quarks are the building blocks of atoms and, as far as we know, the smallest particle in the universe. No matter what the smallest particle is, that particle is the building block of everything in the universe. This building block is the foundation of math, flowers, time, and all living creatures. The natural sequence of numbers is as many as there are quarks since there is no need to count further. We have all the information we need about the universe.

By knowing the number of all building blocks at any given time, we know how much matter there is in the universe at that point in time. By adding or multiplying to this number, we do not get any new information about the universe, so it might be meaningless to do so. In a universe where the balance of energy appears to be total, there might be movement but no time. This conclusion can be reached when we understand that energy cannot be matter but a property that can be found in matter. Deus ex machina, so to speak.

Time could be a way to measure the rate of change of an object or system. In an energy system (universe) with a perfect balance, there cannot be any time measurement since nothing changes. This state of no change will only last for a second or an eternity because nothing wants to be in perfect balance permanently, all things want to evolve and change to reach a higher energy state. This higher state of energy can only be reached when the system becomes first unbalanced and then tries to reach a new and higher state of balance. As a toddler wants to walk, it must stand up and, in so doing, becomes unbalanced.

Time exists in this dimension and is omnipotent because of evolution and matter. Time can be manipulated in higher dimensions because it has a variable's quality. This suggests that one could see and change the future by altering the inputs at the starting point. The starting point for a time traveller in our dimension would be when the time machine was operational, and for someone born in a higher dimension when they were born, but neither can go further back than the starting point without changing their timeline. When travelling back in time one would either switch to another timeline or create a new timeline

One can observe the past but not alter it without creating a new timeline. If one could alter the past, one could go back five minutes after the big bang and move one rock and no earth. No time machine would be built hence a paradox. The paradox only applies to our timeline.

Someone would try to undo creation, and the benevolent universe would let you try to do that. But of course, they would fail, and all would be well, and no paradox would arise. For example, if someone made a time machine five hundred years ago, they could only use their time machine to go forward in time and back to their own time. From our perspective, we would perceive it as they are moving forward and backward in time. This is only because their starting point is before our starting point. As Einstein said, time appears relative to the observer.

Regarding time travel, one could only return to the 'second' after the last time travel began, so that one does not alter the reason for doing the previous travel before it happens. Otherwise, there would not be a return trip to come back from. Going back in time would also require all matter in the universe to move back to that point in time if time is linear. Imagine the energy needed to do that for the whole universe. Time would still move forward for the time traveller, and the point of return or starting point would always move forward. Time measures changes and cannot be turned back or undone as a change has occurred. One can only create a new offshoot to one's own timeline. Time and matter are connected, and one cannot exist without the other. On the other hand, regarding time and metaphysics, here, time holds no dominion. Time cannot be a factor. Only consciousness can.

When physical being becomes aware of this fact, then changes can be made according to one's desires. If those desires can be made to fall in line with the universe, all one's true wishes will manifest in the physical world (after some time, do you know why it requires time to manifest in the physical world?). Regarding Metaphysics, consciousness can be seen as an energy that uses the body's sense organs to translate information from the universe to the mind. The mind can only understand so much, and its limits can limit your worldview if you allow it. The consciousness can be seen as (part energy, part matter) the Vesica Piscis between the soul, energy, and the mind, matter. The energy part consists of the same energy that created the universe.

The soul wants to raise its energy, so that it can together with other souls, rejoin the whole and raise the energy field to a new level. The larger energy system, the 'whole', can be described as non-moving, immutable, and timeless. That which never changes or does not need energy, we regard as eternal. The 'soul' or energy in matter, is a part of the whole, so it appears to be eternal. Souls and consciousness might be the same energy, but regardless of that it animates matter.

The body is, of course, made of matter and, in some regards, the ultimate vessel for the energy that created the universe. We consist of two distinct parts. The soul is pure energy consciousness and incorruptible, the same energy that lit the stars. The body and the mind are made of matter. The two latter can be altered or manipulated positively or negatively. The consciousness is the mediator that mediates and transmutes energy from the whole into matter, and matter from the body-mind into energy. Matter in the body-mind sense includes thoughts, feelings as well as food. We can transform the body and mind by using our consciousness as a medium.

I believe it works like this. If you use your consciousness to predominantly listen to the incoming information from the soul, the all, the universe, or God, you can ultimately have a Buddha-like or Jesus-like consciousness. On the other hand, if you predominantly listen to the information coming from the mind or the physical world, you can ultimately have a materialistic, atheistic, or 'satanical' mindset. We must be incredibly careful about how and what we let our mind focus on, the all, or the ego.

Many organs and body parts function or malfunction depending on inner factors. Thoughts and emotions, for example. Emotions are thoughts that have calcified. This book will not describe external factors, only internal ones. Energy courses through our body, giving it life when in balance and sickness when unbalanced. The body and its organs are vessels for the energy that lit the stars, the soul. This inner energy, universal energy, soul, the void, the silence within, exists in all matter. I believe this energy enables consciousness. When you meditate or go deep within, you will find this silence, the inner void, the ocean in a drop, and you will sense the unlimited power it holds.

Chapter 10

The energy in the inner void can be channelled to heal and alter the mind-body. When you let the consciousness focus on the soul or 'God', the mind-body goes with the flow of that energy. When you let the energy from 'God' or soul flow through your consciousness to your mind-body, it energises the physical world. The more energy you let flow or manifest in the physical world from the soul, will create a feedback loop (lemniscate). More energy goes back to the soul, amplifying it and energising the whole, the consciousness and the mind-body, i.e., the physical world. Energising the physical world, the consciousness, and the whole until the whole is fully charged and can transform that energy into a new universe.

This material universe seems to have material limits as far as we can perceive. There seems to be less solid matter than matter in gaseous form. This is truly fortunate since solids seem to be created from the transformation of gases into solid material. There are several different ways this transformation can be achieved: pressure and heat in combination with an almost absolute freezing point.

Matter is susceptible to external energy. It wants to be influenced. That is why it can be influenced. If it could not be changed by energy, then matter would be timeless and permanent. Hydrogen and Helium constitutes up to 97% of all atoms in the universe. The rest is all other atoms, so why is this, and what happened at the big bang?

In the beginning, there was darkness, silence, and complete stillness, then suddenly a tension that lasted a second of eternity. The explosion of light flooded the empty space and time came into being. At once, movement, light, and sound were present. As the energy dispersed out and around the new space, it slowly cooled, and matter formed. Consciousness was there from the absolute beginning. It was the reason for the event. First, there were only particles as, quarks, neutrons, protons, and electrons. As time passed, pressure, heat, and gravitational forces started to form the first atoms. Hydrogen is the mother of all elements. As hydrogen spread throughout the living space, the conscious hydrogen wanted to evolve, so helium was formed, and gas clouds formed into stars. The stars are the oldest living entities in the universe. When these giants came into being, they wanted to share their song of creation and of the universe, so they shone their light, transmitting their knowledge to all corners of the universe.

Once more, pressure, gravitational forces, sound, and an urge to evolve began to work to create planets. More elements began to form and then compounds. When evolution starts, more 'things' want to evolve, so more objects form. Evolution moves faster as more things come into being. If we look at our own technical evolution, we will see that for many millennia nothing happened. Most of what we have invented was done in the last century. From creation comes diversity, then complexity, and it happens exponentially. Evolution leads to revolution if you let nature run its course. The evolution of an elemental particle, process, or life form is slow initially. The momentum of evolution increases over time as well as complexity.

This is how more things and complex things came into being. Stars, planets, metals, gases, and compounds formed, and finally, physical beings came into being. When consciousness manifests in matter, its natural state is to create and evolve itself and its surroundings. Consciousness is not energy but a movement in energy, it guides and flows with the energy it uses, to manifest its purpose in the universe. Energy is energy and cannot transform into higher, lower, or evolve into another kind of energy. Only matter can evolve to higher or new forms of matter. Matter can become something else, while energy can only change its frequency and or amplitude. Evolution is the only constant in our universe, and all things want and need to evolve.

Energy is used to start this transformation. The energy that exists in every particle makes them self-sufficient in all regards, especially when it comes to the ability to change and evolve. This means that all things and entities have the energy they need to evolve within themselves. No external energy is ever necessary. So as humans, we never need to look outwards for the energy or ability to start the change. We have all that we need within us. If we did not have the energy within us, we would be dependent on external sources. Then there would be a significant risk of scarcity in the universe regarding energy. All matter would be forced to compete for it, creating a situation we seem to experience today on our planet.

All is energy in the universe, which means that all matter holds energy. That energy is in abundance. There is more energy in the universe than there is matter. Energy is the flow of life. Life as we know it can only manifest in matter. Where there is no energy, there is no life. Consciousness is not life because it cannot die. Consciousness is the song in energy, and it sounds like, *Aum*: A, energy in; U, the direction and purpose are selected; M, energy out with direction and purpose.

Chapter 11

Hydrogen can become any atom, and hydrogen is the foundation of all matter. The sun is made of hydrogen (91%) and helium (9%), the most common atoms in the universe. Since hydrogen can and will form all other atoms, there is a lot of matter in the universe or the potential to become matter. All this matter must have some purpose, and we must have a purpose. Is the purpose of matter to come into existence through hydrogen, heat, and pressure to slowly decay into heat energy? Is this our purpose? Is our purpose to transcend to go from matter to, energy beings climbing the ladder higher and higher?

As if it is matter's purpose to become diamonds or some other material as its highest point. If so, what happens after that, eternal bliss, reboot, or nothing? All cells in a specific object constantly reaffirm their position in time and space. If they did not, we would dissolve into clouds of different atoms or become the food we ate. The atoms have strong bonds within themselves, but atoms within an object are not very strongly connected. If atoms were strongly connected within an object, once formed they would be almost indestructible. So why are we stable? What is the reason for this? All things are constantly in flux, changing, transforming, and exchanging their internal parts but keeping their external form. How and why is this happening?

Atoms that leave a body and later join another object bring a residual memory of the first object. In this way, we can say that you know all things in the universe. Since not only did your atoms come from the big bang, but some atoms that joined your physical body bring memories of more recent events. So truly, little or nothing is obscure from us. I do believe that all atoms are connected to all other atoms. They exchange points of view with each other. Consciousness and energy are the fundamental structure of all atoms. If it were not so, I believe that we would not exist. This matter that we are and, surrounds us, what is it for, why do we need it?

If we were pure energy consciousness, we would be one with the creator's consciousness. The need to change or expand our knowledge or experience so that we can evolve would not be a driving force in us. When we came into being, in matter, our purpose must have been very important, why else would we suffer as a human if it was not worth it. As the memory of our purpose slowly fades away, suffering grows. This suffering can become the vehicle for our reason to evolve. We want to reconnect with the wholeness that we came from or create a new wholeness. The only way to do this is to consciously understand and feel this wholeness within us and rediscover our purpose.

In matter, we can achieve this. Matter lets us reconnect with that memory. If we were not in matter, we would be energy and conscious of this wholeness. That makes us not only lucky but also extremely powerful, and our quest in life is the only quest in the universe, and all other activities are mute. Beings from this and other realms want to divert this power from us to themselves, and they have succeeded many times. The illusion we keep on having is that matter is either nonimportant or all-important. If it were unimportant, we would not need it; if it were all-important, we would be trapped in it. Matter is the vehicle we need and use to transform and evolve ourselves so we can know and become part of wholeness. In this regard, it is both none and all-important.

We cannot go anywhere without it, but if we focus on what type of vehicle we are using, we will go nowhere again. All matter in any form is telling us how to reach our destination. If we were to pay attention to everything, it would guide us to the wholeness we desperately seek. Unfortunately, most of us are afraid, unwilling, ignorant, or enjoying ourselves too much to listen. Some people have made this journey, Lao Tzu, Buddha, Jesus, and so on. They tried to impart their knowledge to us in their writings that they left behind. Sadly, we did not understand them, dismissed them, or had them killed for doing this. I believe that many more have made this journey and that we do not know anything about them.

We ignore their message because of fear, fear of change, and fear of reaching our destination before we have enjoyed ourselves thoroughly in the earthly delights. There are many different techniques that people teach each other, so-called necessary techniques to reach this goal, enlightenment. Yoga, meditation, prayer, fasting, and many other techniques are unnecessary because of our higher being. These techniques mainly aim to energise the body and prepare or ease oneself into it. To open up to the universe or the infinite, God or what you want to call it. The irony in going into these techniques is that you already have everything you need. Everything is in place already. You just need to acknowledge it.

The body has a lot of chakras, and they can be used to open you up. There is no question about that. All these techniques do work, but *you do not need them*. How many gurus, enlightened people, or others have used them to reach for the higher planes of consciousness, but no new Lao Tzu, Buddha, or Jesus has come forth? Why? The quest for energy within matter and, to raise it with these techniques becomes empty when one does not know what to reach for. Enlightenment is *not* the end goal. It is just our natural state to be conscious. All matter can transform or become pure energy if the right pressure is applied, but there needs to be a crisis or a longing for something else. A goal cannot be diffuse or unclear, or it will fail.

Most people seeking enlightenment or connection with the source stop there because they cannot see further. They do not dare to dream the highest, most impossible dream that a human can dream, and few realise our creative possibility. Very few go into this search alone.

Most people look for a group that can reassure and validate their struggle and progress. That kind of behaviour is a sure way to not reach your goal since you do not believe that you can do it alone. The ironic part is that you are never alone.

Chapter 12

In matter, there is energy. In atoms, that energy source is active, but in solid matter such as coal, wood, or Water, we define the energy as potential or positional. Energy is energy, so all energy is the same and comes from the same source, which means it is connected. All energy in matter is connected, which means that all matter is connected via energy, which in turn means everything is connected. In the different systems humans have created, there is energy. There is less energy in the physical systems, engines, lamps, and computers than in nonphysical systems like tarot, I Ching, capitalism or communism and ideas.

The latter systems have their highest energy contained in the nonphysical parts. The cards, books, coins, and other objects on which to store the system information has little energy value. The concepts, thoughts, and ideas hold the highest energy value because all of them truly resonate with the universe, even the bad ones. Why is this so? Well, the simple and only answer is everything in the universe, 'good' or 'bad', belongs in/ or to the universe. Nothing is outside of the universe. The idea that gave birth to the atomic bomb holds more energy than the atomic bomb itself.

When we think of energy, most of us think of energy in matter, which is the only energy we tend to believe in and that we can measure. We increasingly believe in energy in thoughts, feelings, emotions, ideas, and concepts. For instance, Nazism has a lot of energy in its religious and ideological form. Although it goes against the fabric of the universe, it still holds the energy of the universe. Buddhism also holds a lot of energy, but its core beliefs do not go against the fabric of the universe. On the surface, they look the same; energy-wise, they are the same. Both hold energy from the universe, and the universe accepts both views. The significant difference is that Nazism tries to force its energy on the universe to 'build' a new universe in its image. Buddhism On the other hand flows with the universe's energy and aims to become the universe in every practitioner.

When we work with the universe, we have all the energy at our disposal, and the energy in the universe is endless. Do you understand why this is? When we go against the universe, the energy that one can access is the energy that one can conjure, take, steal, cheat, or otherwise gather. This is why Buddhism is still a living way of life 2500 years later, and the Nazi empire perished after twelve years. When one flows with the river, you have all the river's energy aiding you. The same goes for our physical machines. If they work with the universe, they will have an endless supply of energy and no unhealthy by-products. But if they work against the universe, they will waste a lot of matter/energy to produce some energy.

When we talk of matter as a source of energy, we are talking about the matter itself and not the energy within the matter. When burning matter to release the energy within, we cheat ourselves out of prosperity and a clean world that does not produce much heat. Matter wants and strives to evolve. In that process of evolution, energy is generated. The substance begins to vibrate, energy levels rise, and at the pivotal moment at which the object evolves, energy is released. This is how nature works with the universe and in harmony with its surroundings so that the whole can benefit and evolve.

I use the term 'harmony' loosely. From our perspective, almost nothing in nature looks harmonious. It is just claws, fangs, and stomachs, but from a higher perspective, it is harmony. The energising of matter is an area of knowledge that many of us understand and find natural because we eat, drink, fall in love, make love, sleep, meditate, and do a host of other things to replenish our energy. All matter is energy. This is so because of the atoms.

But 99% of atoms are empty space, so when we burn coal, we do not burn atoms because they cannot be destroyed, so are we burning empty space? When burning coal, a chemical reaction with oxygen excites the electrons in the atoms, making them spin faster and generate heat, releasing energy. It is the pathways between the atoms that "burn" or dissolve.

When a lump of coal is formed, many carbon atoms bond together by sharing their electrons. These electrons start to travel in pathways between different carbon atoms. These pathways then calcify and create energy bonds. The pathways between atoms are "solid", and when we 'burn' coal, these pathways dissolve and release energy and heat. This is the matter that burns in coal and reduces the mass. When it comes to the brain, it is the same process. Learning and repetition solidify your personality.

How you think creates pathways in your brain, and the more you indulge yourself in that thinking, the harder your personality becomes and solidifies. When we encounter a new way of seeing the world or thinking, these pathways diminish, and energy flows to new pathways. Your world blossoms and you feel good, happy, energised. In some rare instances, old pathways dissolve. This happens when one completely abandons a way of thinking and create a whole new way of seeing the world. These insights can be called enlightenment. When those moments happen, a tremendous amount of energy is released. It is like an atom bomb went off in your mind.

When we read that God made the universe through its word, what is meant by that statement is it that the vibration from the spoken word has created a form, and that form was the universe. The word solidified the energy field into atoms in the universe and created DNA patterns for all objects. This is how the ten thousand things came into being. If one has pure energy and the DNA of an object, all one needs to figure out is how you get the energy to read the DNA, so it creates the object.

No matter is set in stone. All matter wants to evolve. This is the nature of things, but observer bias or discrimination decides what is real. And what is perceived as solid, formed, or static can be repressive for change. A simple example is when a child does not want to follow in her parents' footsteps. The child's will to be its own person is repressed by the parents' bias that the child should be this person because it is the best way, according to said parent. Our beliefs, anticipations, bias, discriminations, or wanting's make objects appear solid or have form. But if one had no beliefs, if you could see an object for what it truly was, that object would be free, formless full of potential as it is, as we all are.

We trap objects and people, in a set form, denying their true nature and potentiality. That is what we do to each other and matter. Matter is loose, not solid. It is open and full of potential, willing to change, that is our and matters true form, formless. Suppose we would see ourselves and matter as something in a state of flux. Always becoming and never solid or formed, the universe would be full of enormous possibilities and mystical miracles, as it obviously is.

Chapter 13

Water will harmonise with the energy frequency of the object it encounters. If we let our minds be subordinate to our perception and consciousness which sees all and knows all, we could be as water, always becoming. Energy behaves like water. It flows to and through the easiest pathways, and obstacles are evaded. Energy as water is life, it has a purpose, and it follows the laws of nature. Our thoughts become energy. What we think, feel, and believe in is energy. The more energy you pour into a thought, belief, or feeling, the more it forms. It becomes increasingly solid, and the idea, thought, belief, or feeling is locked into place. It forms and holds its position to ensure its survival, and subsequent thoughts, ideas, beliefs, and feelings rise from it to expand and support the belief, feeling, or idea.

As above so below. I do believe that all matter was created this way, the same way a thought becomes an idea. When we use energy to create solid objects, regardless of whether those objects are thoughts or things. Objects are not solid but act or appear solid because of our focus on the object. when you give focus and energy to an object it forms and manifests in the physical world. The more focus and energy invested in the object to keep it in place, the more it is perceived as solid. Ideas, recurring thoughts, and feelings are objects we have invested energy and focus on continuously, so they stay in solid form. When we pour energy and hold an object in focus, making it solid, it loses potential because we do not let the energy flow naturally to the lowest point. So that, it can energise and elevate the object to its highest point.

This is using force to manifest a solid object forcing the object to become what we want. To create with power, you give an object energy, care, and focus. Care, in this sense, is the care of wanting a child to find its own path in the world. Force is to give the child the tools you think are needed, to walk a path you think is the best one and, always make sure she stays on the 'right' path. When one forces an object, it loses almost all potential. If one keeps forcing it, the focus strips the object of its potential, forcing it to become one thing, one position, one form. When the object is locked into place, we arrest its development so it appears to be the object we wanted, keeping it in our focus so it cannot change.

This position holding is force, but when we let things, objects be, not determined, in its position, the object can express its inner power. One can act good so that one does not go to prison. Or one can act good because one is good, and prison will never be a force to factor in. Now that we know how to solidify energy into an object, how does one reverse the process, restoring potential and power to that object? Let go of the object, thought, feeling, or idea so it can become neutral and full of possibility. One must release it to the void, the universe. You must let go of your focus on the object. By not focusing on it but still giving it energy and releasing it to the universe, it will once again become a thing with all the potential and power to become what it is supposed to be.

Nice words, right, but how does one really let go of thoughts, ideas, or feelings? A book that can help with that is *Letting Go* by R. Hawkins. What about physical objects like a spoon? How does one let go of that? It is the same method as letting go of thoughts, feelings, and ideas, but the question becomes who is most invested in the spoon being a spoon? Who determines the form of an object, the object itself or the observer? There are three possible ways to look at this.

First, the observer determines the form of an object. This means the object is forced into a position that the observer wants, but this is slavery or external force, so this cannot be right.

Second, the observer and the object tell each other what they see and then agree on what the object is. Internal power and external force join. This is the way for most objects and people today, but not quite right, is it?

Third, the object decides its own form and internal power, and there is no discrepancy between will and fact. External force and influence are impossible with a conscious object or entity, which is the whole point of being conscious, that you can choose your own way or form.

This must be why all objects have a consciousness in the universe, so they can become what they know they should be.

Chapter 14

If consciousness and free will is the basis of life in the universe, then all actions, if conscious, are willing actions. If one would conjure a doughnut out of thin air, the atoms that formed that doughnut were willing to participate in that act. One could influence atoms to come together to form objects. You could even get a group of atoms to evolve into another type of atom if the atoms agreed/wanted to do so. But could you force an atom to become something it did not want to be? In other words, could one force the basic element of the universe and, in so doing, the universe, to do one's bidding? Since the atom and the universe are very conscious, their participation must be conscious and willing.

If the atom or the universe would do something that we, who are not conscious, would perceive as bad or wrong, would it be so? If a comet hits the earth and destroys it, that would be bad on the level of human consciousness, but some of us would be indifferent. Not arrogant indifferent, but neutral because we are all part of the universe, so we never die. They would only be sad that the human experience is ending. If the universe's consciousness finds that earth had its time, then that consciousness cannot be wrong, can it? Can the consciousness that created and maintains the whole physical universe be wrong about anything? If that consciousness can be wrong about anything, it would not be the ultimate consciousness, and any silly little thing could happen to anything in the universe.

Something that is fully conscious will act in a way that is best for the universe, so what is the best path for the universe, is it evolution? So why would evolution be the best and only path that the universe walks? That answer is going to be answered in the last book.

One could influence matter to do one's bidding but one must be conscious. This is the reason it is so important that we become conscious. Otherwise, someone could influence us to become anything they like us to be. We are this consciousness, energy in these bodies, matter that can think and act. Why can matter act, and what are we supposed to act on?

When the formless is made into an object, its original qualities and energy are lost. Moving a formed object back to formless will both make the object rejoice and rise in power. If we could keep energy in a state of potentiality, flux, and uncertainty, it would be possible to form it into any object of matter. Energy has its highest charge just before it determines a direction and discharges. For example, two people meet, and they fall in love; the relationship grows, energy builds up, and they get married: energy is released, and now they have gone from formless to form, Mr and Mrs so-and-so. An unmarried person does this with every new sexual encounter. He or she sleeps with someone, and energy is generated, spark, build-up, and release but never becoming form. Never creating a lasting heartbeat or the *Aum* sound whit the person. The A is the spark, U is the build-up, and M is the release. This does not mean sleeping around with many people is good. It means that you and your partner must find the heartbeat in your relationship, so it does not die.

This advice goes for all relationships. One has friendships, colleagues, and so on. You must find the heartbeat in it, or the relationship flatlines becomes form and stops living. Just before the collapse into reality, energy or an object is at its highest capacity before the release or becoming a form. A formless energy or object will not define anything or anyone. But a formed object wants to and, believe it can define all things, but is that possible. You can read the Buddhist story of 'Zen Master Hakuin' or the Taoist story about a 'farmer and son' to understand the point I am trying to make.

The master Hakuin and the farmer are formless. The other characters are formed, so they form opinions about the farmer and master Hakuin and the events around them. By defining an object, one now proceeds to judge the quality of that object. All lies can be built on the belief of separation of objects. The illusion of defining objects, people, and thoughts is so common that most people believe that it is a natural law or at least a reality that defines our reality. In time there is only one moment that exists, and that is this moment. If this is the only moment in time that exists, then what is memory or matter? Nothing can exist in the past since the past does not exist, but everything might exist in the future. All the unrealised moments are 'soon-to-be-realised' moments or events in the future.

These moments can be laid out as rows of beads to create a timeline, although the definition line is not entirely correct. The timeline is more like a ball of yarn made of many different coloured yarns. Sometimes they intersect. Other times they intertwine. The different coloured yarn does not have the same length, but they all become one in the end. If there are a hundred different colours in the beginning, in the end, there is only one colour, that is, the mix of colours of the remaining yarn.

The future is all these possibilities, all these unrealised moments and events. Ready to come into being, manifesting energy, matter, thoughts, and new possibilities. The past does not exist, time is now, and the future is open to all possibilities. Every moment can be described as a curve. The curve has five distinct points, start build-up, plateau, collapse, and ending. The build-up and collapse are intervals from the start to a plateau and from a plateau to the end. The plateau point is where the moment materialises. It is at this point that this moment and everything exists. One could see the whole curve as a circle where the start and end are at the same point, and time is circular. That circular movement creates a 'timeline', a chain of events that does not leave a trail. It is in the collapse phase where the potentiality begins from the recent moment. Possibilities arise for anything to happen and that blossoms into a new moment.

Interlude The Law of Attraction

Remember, you are an intrinsic part of the universe, and it wants what is best for the universe to evolve into the best version of itself in harmony. If you become the best version of yourself, then a piece of the universe has reached the spot where it is going, which is a good thing. By creating moments and events that make you evolve into the best versions of yourself, you are more likely to help others to evolve. You will be a guide to further the evolution of the universe to its 'goal'.

When you evolve in your consciousness, you will know that good or bad outcomes are interchangeable or the same. They do not differ. One is not better than the other because of the universe and its end goal. Do not mind anything that happens; all is well in the universe, so it is well with you. The universe does not recognise 'good' or 'evil', it strives for balance. When it comes to the law of attraction, there is one thing that we must take into consideration, and that is your consciousness or your higher being. You cannot manifest anything that your consciousness does not find of useful for your journey. If you are conscious of your consciousness, it will block your ability to manifest things that you do not need. You can try to 'attract' whatever your mind wants, but if that does not align with your consciousness. It will not let your mind get what it believes it wants and needs. The mind is immersed in the physical world and has endless things it thinks it wants and needs. Suppose you want to manifest all that your mind wants. You must block out your consciousness and ignore your path in this world. Then you can do or manifest anything.

The universe is like a happy dog playing fetch, and anything that the mind wants it brings, but the consciousness is the gatekeeper. Some of us who are in touch with our consciousness cannot attract something that does not aid us in walking our path. Our life can be perceived as challenging since not much seems to go our way. This is because if we do not walk our own path, we will be stuck in purgatory until we remember and start walking it. When walking our path, we can use the law of attraction to attract things that belong there. And it will be aligned with the universe and our consciousness. Some people seem to know that they need to walk a certain path, others seem to know what that certain path is, and many do not seem to have a path. I believe it is because some listen, some partly listen, and some do not listen to their consciousness at all. People who do not know that they have a path might encourage or discourage those who have one or are looking for one. Find your path or be part of someone else's path.

Chapter 15

Nothing is meaningless in the universe. Things can only be conscious or not conscious. If there is a meaningless object in the universe that does not have any purpose. That would imply that there was no consciousness involved in its creation. The implication goes further, and we arrive at the point that the consciousness of creation is not always conscious, and that cannot be because then the creation would become absurd and collapse. Nothing can be separated from the whole. If it could, then nothing in the universe could be truly whole. As humans, our default state is to be conscious, but we choose to ignore this state, so we become unconscious. An unconscious mind cannot be conscious, as a conscious mind cannot be unconscious. Only a conscious mind can observe and understand an unconscious mind.

Since all things in the universe are in a state of co-creation, symbiosis, and mutual benefit. When we give a wish to the universe, the gift that comes back is to and, for the universe and the giver. The universe and you will enjoy seeing the wish come to fruition because you and the universe are a part of the whole, and everything in it will benefit from your wish. What about egotistic or even evil wishes? Are they to be enjoyed by the universe even if they do not help the whole but only a separate part? Of course not. A gift based on the separation from the whole will not be granted, but it might materialise if enough force is applied to the wish, see dictatorships, Islamic State (Isis), Nazism, and so on.

Evil actions materialise because enough force is applied to see them come to fruition, but it cannot work against the whole for a very long time. Killing a person or a nation does not mean the event is bad. The bad thing is that you might create imbalance in the universe. But we cannot be the judge of that. One's gift of potentiality to oneself and the universe should not be a wish that creates events leading to an 'increasing' imbalance. Those wishes one must work hard to realise. To go against nature, your higher being, and of course, the universe.

The universe will not stop you from realising your wish, no matter how bad it is, if you and others put enough energy into it. There are two ways one can manifest things in this universe. You can ally with the universe and let it do the heavy lifting, and it will be enduring and easy. Or you can go against or not trust the universe and do it yourself, working hard to realise your wish, but it will be short-lived. Although God, the whole did create separation, when the universe was created because there cannot be wholeness without separation. Sickness, greed, and hate are all signs of imbalance. They are the result of ignoring balance. If one truly felt and knew that balance/wholeness is the state of all things in the universe, including oneself, nothing would happen to you without your permission. Because of the simple fact that if you are conscious your permission is the all's permission.

All things that are made of matter know and feel this wholeness. It knows it is a point of view of the all, a unique view that allows the universe to transform itself. This unique view is that we are everything in the universe. All these different perspectives become a holistic way of seeing itself. This holistic view of the universe can only happen when all parts are conscious about themselves and their view. When that happens, the universe can become a new wholeness. God or the whole created duality for our benefit so that we could realise that we were a part of the whole, to reach that conclusion we must feel separated from the whole/God. We knew when we came in to matter that we would feel separated from the whole, we needed that contrast to create. The ego or mind just amplifies that feeling, especially when we do not know our purpose for coming here. The feeling of separation makes us suffer; use the suffering you feel to find your purpose. Whatever your mind believes in becomes 'real' in the world unless you are conscious.

Hard and soft, cold and hot, and fast and slow are essentially vibrations and rhythm. The duality that we perceive is just fluctuations in the field of energy. These fluctuations are 'stable', which means that we perceive the phenomenon as a separate state, although they are not in reality. In all planes of existence, everything sits in a sea of energy. Everything is energy. Our planet sits in this sea of energy. This sea of frozen energy behaves like water; things move through it, and there can be waves, ripples, and displacement. The energy field around our planet and all other planets are different from each other, and the field is different around the planets than in empty space. Every planet vibrates differently due to its composition, making them unique, like a person. When the energy field moves, different galaxies, solar systems, and planets react differently to that movement.

You can equate the energy field with water and movement in the energy field like a wave in water. The planets, in this case, are rocks in the water. After hitting a rock, the waves will disperse a certain way. Every rock will disperse the incoming energy differently and absorb it differently because of its unique composition. Certain waves can move or even break a rock, but another rock will be fine if that wave hits it. Like people, we react differently to incoming energy because of our mental composition, and the output is also different. Everything in this universe is a co-creation with everything else, so everything becomes an observer and the observed, the giver and the receiver, the active and the passive. This is described as Yin and Yang by the Chinese.

A lie is an immensely powerful thought to engage in and has more energy than the truth. One cannot, without consequence, build on a lie. One must constantly adjust and amend the lie. In the end, that house of cards will crumble. If we observe the world, societies, and people today, it seems that we are missing the point. Only the most invested in the lie strongly oppose the search for truth. A lie can only shrink one's world and never expand it. Truth always expands the world. When we unconsciously decide what an object 'is', we trap both parties in a lie, and neither can expand beyond that lie. The lie affects both parties. Equally, I cannot define you if you do not define me. By accepting each other's lies, we can act on our own lies about the other and ourselves. By accepting only some characteristics of ourselves and others, we trap each other in a shallow shell that we call the self. If we do not define anything, we cannot be defined and are free to become anything at any moment. This applies especially to humans and other sentient beings.

When religious or spiritual people talk about God, they do it in a way that often baffles the non-believer. God is often described as singular, unique, unreachable, and as a consciousness that became conscious by itself. An entity in isolation that became the supreme consciousness, but is this the case? If we look at matter, matter cannot develop without other matter, and an atom cannot become something else without input or influence. When separated from the whole, there cannot be any evolution, so our creator must have been in its whole to evolve into our creator. Complex compositions create more complex entities and objects that evolvs. The amoeba is more complex than the composition of the different atoms it consists of.

A computer is complex, but not in comparison to the amoeba. The energy the amoeba creates and flows in it makes it more complex. God made the universe and is still making it. From the universe, all other things are made, but made by and of the universe, via God. God is the divine spark, the source of all things but not the direct creator of all things. I believe God's will is that all beings with a awaken consciousness come to know God and how it created the universe. The reason for this is so that we can expand love and life itself. There is no greater meaning for matter or being if one does not expand love and life to its fullest ability. To just live, love, and work is honourable for the lowest of unconscious creatures, but it holds no real value when consciousness is present.

We must strive for more without strife. In us, all possibilities and knowledge of the universe and God exist. If we ignore all or most of it, we will repeat this life to remember and know our purpose. When we do not reach, for this knowledge, we sin against ourselves, the universe, and God. It is not a serious sin but a quiet one that will lead us to a hollow existence that lacks the flavour of life and true love. Life will be monotonous and filled with activities that mean nothing and which erode our life to an unbelievable bore. That life will push us into activities that are pointless and sometimes dangerous to life, love, and nature for us and our environment.

We must seek this source, whatever it might cost us, no price is too great for seeking it, but the cost for not seeking it is an endless pain. So why do most of us not seek this source when all signs are there, all around us all the time? Why do we not dare when we see it or persist in our quest when we do find the path? Why do so many of us fail? Is the material world so strong and so deceptive that we cannot look at the centre of our hearts and the universe to discover the truth about all things? Why are all these trivial matters and activities so alluring to us when the whole universe and all its knowledge are just a heartbeat away. Why is it so hard to see the path and stay on it? Do we not realise its power, potentiality, and truth? Do we not want to see it? Do we not want to become the master of our own life? What or who is stopping us from living an excellent life as a creator, this is the question we must answer, or we will be trapped in a pointless, boring life.

In my quest for source, I have noticed that the material world is alluring but not to the degree that I want to stay in it since the pain is too great. But still, I do not dare let go, for the fear that I will lose in this game of life. I am still afraid that all the knowledge of the universe and God is less important than money, fame, or whatever I desire. Still, I know this is a horrible lie, but why is this lie stronger and more real than the truth? Is it that I have invested time and energy in convincing and continue to convince myself that the lie is 'real'? The truth, on the other hand, is just there for the taking. No effort is needed. I just have to discard the lie and walk the path of truth. Why am I so afraid that I will lose, surrender or admit defeat in the material world? Is it because the spiritual path is so unclear, and almost everyone seems to fail on it? Why am I so afraid that I have taken the wrong path when I know in my heart that this path is the only one to walk?

Why do I think I have made a mistake when that is impossible? When it feels so right, why do I think it is wrong? Every step makes me feel better, stronger more loved than I have ever felt before, but still, I doubt. That this is the right path. Why do I 'know' it is difficult to make it when it is the simplest thing to achieve? I already have all the necessary parts and knowledge, but I do not believe in it still. Not believing infects all my knowing, thinking, and feeling so that I become a static dead creator, an NPC in life, not creating, only reacting to life. Everything has been tried before fasting, in sex, food, thoughts, and human interactions, but still, almost all of us fail. Where are we going wrong? Why are we failing?

Is it drugs we need? What do we need to step out of our learnt behaviour and think about our true nature? How do we succeed in this? How do I realise that the truth about myself is true, that the power and knowledge we all hold are real and true? How do we put it to beneficial use for humanity and the universe? This knowledge is so tangible and transitory that we lose it when we grasp it. It is like we truly cannot believe it is real, which is why it always floats away, but how do we make it real? Intellectually I know that I am one with the creator, universe, and everything around me, but I dare not act like I am. I hesitate and think and feel that I am not part of this wholeness. Emotion is stronger than intellectual thought. This thought that we are one with God seems to have little basis in the real world. So once more, what matters, and why is the material world so strong that we cannot break free from its hold over us?

As I said earlier, matter is, moving energy that forms patterns and solidifies so we can touch it. Ergo, matter is energy with a specific pattern that we can predict. Everything in the universe is energy, and some of it is energy that has a specific pattern, and it is this that traps us. When our consciousness is in nonphysical form, our energy is free and unbound, and all power and potentiality are available. But if this is so, why did our consciousness come here in matter? Why not stay in nonphysical form and create from there? I do believe that in nonphysical, one does not want to create, but only to be, bask in the glory and love of God. When the wish to create arises when we are nonphysical, it is because we want to evolve to a higher state. Still, the prerequisite for this evolution is that one goes into matter and 'forgets' all the knowledge of creation and God.

To evolve to this higher state, one must rediscover this power, knowledge, and love for God, the universe, and creation. If you fail on the first try, you can repeat the journey into matter until you complete the 'test' and evolve. We are not trapped or too focused on matter and the material world. We are more like a child who, bright-eyed for the first time, visits an amusement park and marvels at the sights and sounds around her. Some techniques can be used to break free from the hold that we believe matter has on us, and you already know of them. I cannot stress enough the value of having a daily meditation practice and keeping alcohol and meat consumption to a minimum, which will help reaching the whole.

Certain drugs can help us on our way; they help us see the nonphysical plane but only in glimpses and fractions, and they can be very confusing and sometimes scary to experience. Most people experience a feeling of being part of the wholeness or universe, God, and they can lead us to the expansion of the mind if we do not abuse them. As many religions point to the way certain drugs make us experience the physical world and know that there is a way out. Or is it in to seek and explore, but we must be careful so that we will not fall into them and let them take us on a ride? These plants were formed on this planet to help us evolve, but the question is why and how they came here. Remember, nothing is coincidental. Everything has a purpose. Terrence and Dennis Mckenna had a great theory called the 'Stoned Ape Theory'. They hypothesised that those early humans ate psychedelic mushrooms that 'grew' the brain, which would account for how our brains grew so fast in a short period of time, and there is some evidence for this.

If everything is connected to each other, there must be a mutual benefit for this exchange. We get a revelation from it, but what are we giving them? The gifts they give us are great and powerful, but why do they choose the form they come in? What do they want us to do with these gifts and knowledge they give us? Do they want us to evolve, but why, and are they benevolent? Anyone who wants to change and evolve another has motives, and those motives can be egotistical. If humans and certain plants did co-create together for the evolution of man, what do the plants get out of it? Why do they want to evolve us? These plants seem to have a direction and a voice, but what direction and whose voice is it? Are the voices ours from the future and the direction forward? I believe that we are being guided from the future and not pushed from the past. Because the past does not exist, the universe does not care what has happened, or is going to happen. It only cares about fulfilling its purpose. In this statement, everything in the universe is equally full of potentiality and hope since everything wants to evolve to its highest form.

But if we are being guided from the future to manifest a certain outcome, what and who is guiding us? It cannot be God; that would negate free will. I believe our future children are guiding us toward them somewhere in the far future, but for what reason? This notion implies that there is an outcome that our distant children do want to manifest, that they consider 'optimal'. Evolution always strives to produce the best version of an object or entity in a specific environment. The outcome they are aiming for must be the best they can imagine. One does not require much energy to create a 'bad' future, that is relatively easy to accomplish.

Chapter 16

If our future children sit on the front row watching the universe collapsing in on itself to be born again, they need to guide their ancestors through the pitfalls and dangerous parts. Perhaps many different futures are trying to manifest as in a competition. One future where we are totally separated from ourselves, nature, and God, one where we are in the middle, and one where we are totally connected whit ourselves, nature, and God. Both God and nature might not care which of these realities is manifested. God does not mind since everything is as it should and will begin anew, and nature does not mind so long as it fulfils its purpose: evolution.

Maybe all these possible futures are competing for attention, pick me, pick me they say, and the one that seems most alluring at the time gets picked, and slowly we start to manifest that future. There is a war in the universe regarding humankind, and it is about our future and how it will be heaven, hell, or death. All futures are acceptable for the universe, so we need to decide what we prefer. On this road to somewhere, some nodes need to be reached on these different paths. Until a crossroad and, then one future is nearer than the others, our choices and consciousness will determine our actions. In every moment, we have to choose how our future will be. We must be conscious and in contact with the universe, the Dao. Every moment is important; there is a war in every moment, and your universe will burn, stagnate or flourish depending on your choice.

Matter is our proxy weapon of choice. We use matter to guide the energy within us to create a future. We get led by the universe and the future we intend for. It will lead us to the future we need and want, but it makes us look like fools and slaves, not free. This is an illusion our ego creates for us, and the truth is that if we follow the universe, we are free. To be and do the most fulfilling actions that our hearts desire, the one who follows the Dao is the eternal slave. This is one of the reasons that Satanists call Christians stupid and slaves to God. Still, another reason is that religion has so many unnecessary rituals that do not guide us to the universe, ourselves, the Dao, or God but bind us to the religion.

The more one participates in the rituals. The more one gets bound to the religion. Some even say that the root word for religion comes from the Latin word *'ligare'*, which means to bind or connect. The whole point with rituals is that they cannot be questioned. They should only be followed without thought, making us unconscious. The ritual becomes more important than the connection to God. I would argue that the point of certain religions is to disconnect us from ourselves, nature, the universe and God, to bind us to the religion, i.e., matter. Religions that tell you what to do and when to do it are false, and those faiths that do not are true to the universe, yourself, nature, and God. So how do we train or prepare ourselves for this? All the usual ways work. Meditation, yoga, focus exercise, mushrooms, ayahuasca, breathing, letting go, journalling, and physical training, you name it and do it.

Keep the body and mind in shape but do not forget why you are doing it. No one can teach you anything. You just need to remember what you already know. Who can tell you what your purpose is, what you should, can, or cannot do, or how to do it? No one can tell you anything significant about yourself or the universe that you don't already know. Everything in the universe is connected, so you are connected to everything. Since everything is connected and known by you, we only choose not to acknowledge this. Ignorance is our bondage. Looking for knowledge outside of ourselves is false. You can only look outside of yourself for clues or pointers to knowledge. This might help you, search your memory and look for the pointers. They will unlock that part of the knowledge it pointed to, and you will understand.

Most of us try to understand information without looking for the knowledge behind the information. Without searching our hearts and connecting to our higher self, this is the reason we do not go beyond our ego. Look at this book, search for the knowledge behind the information, and evaluate the knowledge in your heart. Scrutinise it with your higher self, and the meaning will be yours. If you do not, it will be another book with pretty words and interesting thoughts but devoid of meaning. All these words and thoughts in this book mean nothing if you do not derive meaning and truth from yourself, and to do that, you must go inside of yourself, into your heart and higher being, to see and feel and understand the meaning and truth in the words. These words and thoughts only point to the truth. They are not the truth. They are only an inadequate description of the truth, a pointer to knowledge.

Chapter 17

About 70% of the world and our bodies consist of water, we will die without it in 3-4 days, and all living things consist of and, need it to survive. So, is water just another substance in the universe? Yes and no: we will mostly deal with the no part in this book. Water is made up of two hydrogen atoms and one oxygen atom. Two gases join to create a weird liquid that has three stages within a 100°C span, solid at -0°C, liquid at 1-99°C, and gas at 100°C. It has an anomaly point at 4 degrees Celsius. Here water has its highest density. Therefore, the bottom of lakes does not freeze. What has water to do with our quest or journey? Well, water is a medium. There is a reason Jesus and others were baptised in water, and many holy places are connected to water. Many myths have water as a central theme, such as the sword in the lake 'Excalibur', Titicaca, Atlantis, and so on. Water is, in many cultures, holy and sacred.

There are many instances where water is seen as sacred in the Nag Hammadi texts. It is in the primordial waters where mankind is conceived. Water is not holy because it keeps us alive. If it were so, many things would be holy. The ancient people understood that water had properties that were mystical in nature. The water we see, smell, touch, and enjoy drinking is essentially the same water our ancestors have seen, smelt, touched, and drank. There is a direct connection between them and us, which is water. Water is the medium for all that ever lived, live, and will live on this planet. It will record and remember everything it touches. Its knowledge is supreme on earth. We can ask water anything, and it will answer. Is the knowledge we have a remembrance of what the water in our bodies gave, is giving us? Do we know all about earthly matters because water knows all?

Do we know things, or do we only have information? The earth is round, the clock reads 16:33, and I am facing due south. All these statements can be information or knowledge. Information is not from you or has not been processed by your heart and higher being. The information that the earth is round is what 99% of other people say, but how do you know it's round? (By the way, it is round 100%, no doubt about that). If everybody were saying that the earth was flat, would you disagree? Most likely not, and this applies to most of our 'knowledge' (information). Why is that? If you spent three days in a dark place with no sunshine or watch, and then stepped out somewhere between eleven and four o'clock, could you tell if it were morning, midday, or afternoon and what direction you were facing, or would you need someone to give you that information? If the person providing the information was incorrect or lied, could you decide it was incorrect? If not, what does that say about you or us as people?

Wise people should know the distinction between the ordinary mind and timeless awareness. In our case should know the distinction between information and knowledge. The people who have revolutionised our thinking could see, feel, and know that the phenomenon they described was knowledge, and the old way of thinking was information. They took a subject they felt was wrong, contemplated, meditated on it, did some intellectual work, observations, and so on. Processed it in their hearts and higher being and saw that what was revealed was knowledge, not information. You can be easily misled if you frivolously trust that all information presented to you is rooted in knowledge.

Water always seeks the lowest point. Why is that? The lowest point is the darkest and coldest point. It is here that water can rejuvenate itself and then rise to new heights. Without water, no life. Therefore, we look for water when we look for life in space. If we find water, it may indicate the presence of life. Sunlight and water are the two creative forces on this planet. The substrate they use to create, is carbon and oxygen. When these four get together, then things start to grow. One observation that has been made is that when these two forces meet directly without the substrate, negative things grow. The energy from these two life-affirming sources becomes too powerful when they interact directly. Killing or corrupting life or turning it into something corrosive to life. They need a substrate like carbon, oxygen, cold, and darkness. The substrate acts as a buffer for the powerful energy that water, and sunlight put out so that they will not destroy life. This resembles the Yin and Yang symbol.

These two powers are dualistic in form, heaven-sun-male and earth-water-female, so how do we translate this information into knowledge? The heaven-sun-male is our will or thoughts, earth-water-female is our higher being and heart, and the substrate is time. When the female is in harmony with the male, time is reduced to a minimum. The female must be in total harmony with the male before any creation can be done. The same principle applies to sunlight and water. This is because the female is the more powerful of the two. The female is connected to the universe, and God. It is in the female that all things get created and grow. When harmony is reached between the two energies, the seed will start to grow immediately. If there is an imbalance, the growth will be delayed until the imbalance has ceased, or the seed will die.

To grow a plant, one must be a good and thoughtful gardener who understands the importance of balance between water and sunlight. Water changes temperature in proximity to land, so lakes, coves, and bays have higher water temperatures than open seas. At sea, one could track changes in water temperature to follow warmer water to land. I think this could apply to space travel as well. There must be changes in space that would indicate both a planet and a planet full of life.

Water holds the highest and lowest points since it has no will. It will become what it needs to be and fulfil its purpose by fulfilling all other's needs. If we could be as water and hold any position without judgment or opinion, only with service to others in mind. We would be an unstoppable force of nature for humanity and the earth itself. The water molecule is built like a triangle, the second form in the universe, the first being the circle, which water forms in its smallest part, the droplet. Some people claim that it is from the water droplet that the ancient Egyptians discovered the centimetre. The evidence is incomplete at best, but I find the thought compelling. The sun's energy is made of hydrogen. When the sun's rays and energy meet water or hydrogen in any form, it stimulates the hydrogen into a higher vibration, 'creating' and releasing more energy than in the beginning state.

Hydrogen is the sun for all other atoms and molecules. The hydrogen initiates action and growth in particles, substances, etc. All things are dependent on it. Hydrogen is the root of the energy state in water. In fact, it is the root of the energy state in all substances. If a substance lacks or has a small hydrogen content, it also has a small energy content or is almost devoid of energy. Coal has little energy potential in its purest form, the diamond. If you combine carbon with hydrogen, there is a lot of energy to be used. If you looked at different substances that contain hydrogen, you would notice that the energy potential goes up when it has a high concentration of hydrogen. Hydrogen in water is the portal to all the different stages of water and the path to the core of the material universe. Hydrogen is the building block of the universe, the original atom, and one can reach the foundation of creation with hydrogen.

Oxygen's role is to act as a lubricant, intermediary, and partner so that the hydrogen can regulate its energy outlet and morph or transform water into different states. Water can be described as liquid sunshine where the oxygen ensures that the hydrogen gas is rendered harmless, nonexplosive. When we burn hydrogen with oxygen, we get water. Since water is made of oxygen and hydrogen, where hydrogen is both the primordial atom and the main energy atom, this means that water is not only the substance that is the basis of our life, but I suspect that it is the basis of all life in the universe. Our blood is about 90% water, and our bodies consist of 70% water, so we are mostly made of liquid sunshine or energy. This energy can of course, be directed, repurposed, or transformed into whatever you like.

Water's natural set point is low and where it contains its highest energy, in darkness and at 4 degrees Celsius. In this state, it can become or reflect any energy pattern. By becoming blank or calm in one's water, we can become any energy pattern we choose. We must become like the ocean. All rivers flow to the ocean; in and, all things are born from the ocean. When we become the same energy wave that the ocean is, we become indefinite, formless form. We become all potential that ever existed, and nothing or no one can define us. We become true water. Water is being, non-being, formless form, living life, dying death, becoming and non-becoming, directionless direction. It is all of this and none of this. All water is in flux. Nothing in water is fixed. There is no point of reference, no beginning or end. We do not know where the wave begins or ends. There is no uncertainty to see or understand.

In the ocean, abundance is generated in the dark, deep down, and far away from sunlight. What we see on the surface or in shallow waters is the product of this generated in deep, dark waters. The reflecting light is our material life on the surface, the waves, jetsam, and flotsam. The deep, dark waters are our true self, the immortal, incorruptible, oneness with the universe, soul. If we become like the deep dark waters, our surface would become synchronised with the Dao, or the all. When we become that, we could ask the universe to raise experiences, wealth, ideas, or anything one wished from the deep waters for our evolution. This is what we do when we wish something to happen, and then it does. The 'law of attraction', but we only connect briefly to the deep waters. Things on the surface come from the deep but also from external sources, both 'good and bad things', and you can collect them according to your preferences, so make sure you know what you want.

The universe, i.e., *you*, will create anything for us, and it will let you rendezvous with it if you let it. There is nothing the universe will not create for you, but it will create it where, when, and how at its own discretion. You can trick a lot of people but not yourself or the universe. One important question is, what do I want? If you utterly understand that you can synchronise with the universe, the

Dao, and that you can have anything you like in the universe, what would you ask for? Think about this question for a while: What would you ask for when you could have anything you like? To disappoint you a bit, most people who reach this stage in their development do not ask for anything. They are content with being alive and gently enjoying life. Watching time and the universe pass by, smiling and laughing at the beautiful universe dancing to its own rhythm. Water moves like the Dao, and it can teach us how to connect with ourselves and sync with the universe.

Water has its highest energy potential when at rest, and the temperature is 4 degrees Celsius. Here, we can move it in a certain way so that it generates energy. In this state, it will cleanse itself from impurities and is the best source of clean energy for all living things. When water is in this state, it will influence other materials, energising them. Water will even energise metals. This could be called cold energy, and it does not use oxygen to burn the hydrogen but to cool it. The oxygen holds the hydrogen in place, so it stays liquid, allowing the hydrogen to generate excess energy. This energy process resembles electromagnetic energy. The two hydrogen atoms revolve around the oxygen atom, trying to connect to each other, to become dihydrogen. The oxygen molecule cools this process down, but more oxygen is needed to keep the process cool. A water molecule revolves around another water molecule creating a higher charge. The entire process is also regenerative, so if one uses the energy, it will continue to generate energy as long as you add oxygen. The oxygen keeps the process stable and regenerative by cooling the hydrogen, preventing it from becoming gas and igniting.

The oxygen atom gets "spent" during the process and needs to be replaced. Oxygen lubricates and cools the hydrogen so that the hydrogen can generate energy without combustion. When the water in a stream flow downhill, it knows with 100% certainty that it will reach the lowest point of the sea, co-creating and benefitting all things that it passes on the way. So be like water: co-create, serve all, and seek the lowest position, and you will reach the sea. Oxygen is the medium combustion use to burn hydrogen, and carbon is the facilitator of combustion, but carbon is not a great energy source. Oxygen is a lubricator for many different substances. Carbon is the facilitator for growing organic life, while HOC (Hydrogen, Oxygen, and Carbon) is the building block of life. In every drop of water, there is a river, an ocean, and a vortex. Water's own nature wants to flow, reach the deepest point, form an ocean, be a current, a wave, and be abundant. It is in the DNA of water to be this thing.

If we look at a drop of water, one will see the ocean, waves, rivers, currents, and vortexes. You would see a universe in that drop of water. A river may begin 2000 metres underground, and a wave may begin on the other side of the ocean, but just as the river will find the ocean, the wave will find the shore. It is their purpose. We have a purpose, and if we act, think, and behave like water, our purpose will come to us naturally so that we can fulfil it. Sidenote this is what evil people and Satanists call slavery because, from the outside, it looks like you do not have free will or a choice since purpose seems so predestined, or are they right? Are we slaves to God's will when we have a purpose?

There is no free will if the universe and sentient beings are separated from God. Then we only do what we are programmed to do (see animals) if God has a specific purpose for every individual and the universe and enforces it on us. Why create the universe and us only to turn it into a puppet show? Is it free will if you and your mind decide what purpose you should have and then set out to execute it? How does your purpose fit in with the universe and the rest of humanity? How do you know where you begin and your culture ends? If you do not know, then do you have free will? All the beliefs, thoughts, and knowledge that society and people have given you, bind your thinking, ergo, your free will, binding you to a time and place. You do not have free will if you cannot see past them. You are only executing your programming.

In the Bible, the angels must follow God's commands, and it is this that the devil rebel against. The angels do not have free will in this story, but can you spot the inconsistency? If the angels did not have free will, how could they rebel? Free will is given to all beings since all beings are connected to the source, so we are one. So why would we control ourselves to get a certain outcome from the universe and humanity, if we were there at the moment of creation together with God? Why would God go through the motions of having us play out a 'movie' that God already knows the ending of? That seems like a very human thing to do.

We are water drops in the rain. We fall from heaven and experience separation, an illusion that continues as we fall to the ocean. And in the ocean, we begin to slowly rise to the heavens to do it all again. Our lives are lived in the rivers. They start in the heavens, fall to the mountains, go down into the river, and travel to the ocean to rise again, so we need to trust in ourselves and source. In the river, we will meet all the experiences that life in matter has to offer. The clearer our water drop (wisdom or knowledge about oneself) is, the more knowledge we will derive from these experiences. By having self-knowledge, you are contributing to the purification of your river and, in turn, the ocean. The purpose is to make the river and, ultimately, the ocean as clear as the source in 'heaven' so that they become identical, heaven on earth. The ocean or source on earth appears murky or obscure, so we have a tough time seeing and feeling source. This is because how we perceive the universe, matter is the only thing we can trust. That matter is obscuring the living energy in it, due to our limited beliefs and perception.

Chapter 18

As energy is in everything, it also connects to everything. When everything is connected, why do you not feel this connection? "Behind the veil" means to see source in its true form as we can perceive it. What we must do in our lives is to reach beyond the veil to let source in matter meet source. While we are in matter, we must fully understand in our conscious mind that our part of source is the bridge between matter and source. When the connection is made, that bridge will stay there. The work for sentient beings in matter is to form more connections with source so that the veil is lifted. The Buddha and Jesus are two who made this connection; there have been many more who have done this.

When we take certain substances, we temporarily make this connection, but it will only last as long as the high last, and then the memory of the connection diminishes. This is very significant that we make these temporal connections. Unfortunately, most of us get so starstruck by the experience that we do not recognise what we need to do. We might think we have to use a substance to go beyond the veil. Substances only work if we have receptors that can process them. This means that you are the one that facilitates the connection. The substance is the trigger, and makes the connection last longer and stronger, but we could train ourselves to make these connections. Many of us have had flashes of this without substances, so one can train oneself to make this connection at will and, make it last for as long as needed.

We made these connections even when we did not intend to. Or we make the connection when we adapt to spirituality. We also do it in dreams and when we let go of our ego, often in times of great distress. Most of us do not know what we experienced when we connected in those moments, so we might dismiss it as a weird thing or a profound vision. The problem is that we often place the experience outside ourselves and do not even think we can reproduce it. In any case, we made the connection without the substance indicating that we are the ones that created this connection at will, and we could do it again with training.

When we struggle with spiritual teachings, we often do not ride the wave of understanding. This means we do not recognise the incoming information or know how or what to make of it. What I think most of us do is think, 'with what knowledge do I question my old knowledge?' It is hard to incorporate new knowledge into our Corpus Hermitica in our minds. This especially applies to those without a physical teacher or guide to aid in the spiritual journey. It is extremely hard to know what information one is supposed to learn and from whom. I am using the word information because before you have processed it in your heart so that it can become knowledge, it is just a bit of information, just as this book is just information before you have made it into knowledge.

I have often discarded information at first but later found it to be crucial for my development. Or the opposite, a bit of what I thought was very important knowledge was information or even a lie. There are many teachers out there, past and present, who, just as I am, claiming to be unbiased, good, and telling the truth. Is there any difference between them and me? Honestly, I do not know. No. Maybe or yes, there is a difference between other writers of spirituality and me. That depends on a few things, such as the writers' intentions and knowledge, the reader's ability to understand and transform information into knowledge, and whether the information is true or not.

I have distilled knowledge from many diverse sources in this book and the two that will follow. From all that knowledge, I have derived meaning that is universal but specific to my purpose. My books have nothing to teach. I have nothing to give you in the way of knowledge or understanding. I am writing a journal about how I came to my conclusions. How I was guided to understand what I needed to understand so that I could do what I always was supposed to do. This non-action that I have already done demanded enormous amounts of preparation. It needed knowledge, energy, guidance, and of course love, before I could successfully perform it, and this is what these books are all about.

It is just a journal, no more, no less; what knowledge I impart you already have. These books are not a recipe for you to follow but an account of how I did it so that you will know with certainty that you can also do it. How you reach your conclusions and knowledge is your journey, and my journey has nothing to do with yours. We always have teachers, guides, and masters who aid us in our journey. You are never alone. Source is Omnipresent, of course, but it is hard to detect and decode the beautiful messages that your higher being, the universe, and source send to you to encourage you to go on. But not all voices are there to help or support. Some voices have their own agenda, and one can easily go astray or get caught up in a web of lies and misinformation. It is imperative that you know yourself and develop an intuitive and critical thinking mind, and above all else, become conscious so that your mind listens to your heart, it will save time, and it can save your life.

Is material wealth something to strive for? The answer is yes, and no. Getting or having material wealth may not diminish your spiritual work or being. But it often makes one attached to the trappings of material world. Your focus is directed towards it, and you start to equate your worth and life with it. So how does one deal with this attachment? In the same way, you deal with all attachments. You let them go. Remind yourself that this wealth does not really mean anything. Money has no true value. It is the agreement that it has a value that is the energy or value of money. It is we, the people, who grant money this value. If we disband this agreement, that money no longer has any value, just think of the Deutsch mark 1920-1930, the Zimbabwe dollar, 2010. If most people agree that what you own is desirable and holds value, it holds value. If they change their minds, your material wealth will disappear. Matter does not hold value. Only what we as people decide to focus our energy on, holds value.

Knowing this simple truth makes it easier for me to detach from material wealth but also easier to attract it to me since it has no true value to me. It only has practical value for me. Money was agreed upon in antiquity to easier facilitate trade. I could show up with a bunch of silver coins instead of a hundred fish, ten pots, and a deer antler to trade for that canoe I wanted. Practical, yes, but only so long as everybody else saw value in my coins. The same holds true today, but money's energy or value seems overlooked or forgotten. When we treat money for what it truly is, straw dogs or practicality notes, our obsession with money dissipates. Nonmaterial wealth is far more powerful. Most people value their inner wealth or truth more than material wealth. Which one do you prefer, true love or bought love?

According to the accounts, two of the world's most known holy men, Buddha and Jesus, had vastly different experiences of material wealth. Buddha was born into material wealth, and one could claim that it was a prerequisite for his ascension. On the other hand, Jesus was born into relative poverty, which seems to be his prerequisite for ascension. But money is way down the list if we make a list of things we need to survive. Why do we not use the most or second most valued material for humans? Air and then water are the most valued materials for us humans. Without them, life would be brief. Both exist in abundance on earth, making them not desirable from a monetary viewpoint, and they are also ridiculously hard to store and carry around. But you get my point, so why is this obsession with money, gold, and other energy storage methods? It makes the barter of goods and services easier. That's it.

Money is an energy conserver and accumulator that lets you decide when and where you want to be resource strong. Money is not energy, nor can it bring you happiness, knowledge, or wisdom. Money is barely even matter now (digital currency). It is a powerful idea in our minds that we are obsessed with. The agreement is that whatever we designate as money is valuable to all in that system. I do think that most of us would like to see this agreement nullified and that money abolished. Because who would want that something so arbitrary as money would be so important to and for my life? Our ideas and creativity might have value with a money-based system. One does not need consciousness in a money-based system. Everything can be motivated by profit; in many regards, it is. What do you think you could trade a fidget spinner with if there was no money? What value do you think we would assign to it?

What would happen if we agreed that ideas and creativity were of value? What would our currency be? Cooperation, compassion, advancement of the human mind and soul. Something connected to creativity and ideas. In that world, could one build anything knowingly harmful to nature, animals, or humans? Could ideas that would cause harm to us, be accepted? Ideas and creativity require thought and heart to interact for both the creator and the observer. One can fool oneself but not everyone. Money has no morals, nor does it require the user to have morals. But ideas and concepts that we want people to believe in tend to have a moral code. These moral codes must be internalised by the intended members and must be consistent with the previous moral codes of the members. But those moral codes must be in sync with life, nature, love, health, and freedom in order to be a yardstick for what morality is. If one lacks these qualities, then the moral of an idea might not be deduced, for example, communism and nationalism. A lot of people still cannot deduce the flawed moral in these two ideas, maybe because they are money-based ideas.

Water does not need or want to be moved since the essence of water is movement. It moves within itself. We, humans, are similar. We do not need other people for ascension. It might feel easier if help is given, but we do not need it. All one need is oneself and a consciousness (which we always have), and as perception 'grows', so does freedom. After a while, our choices are reduced to walking in truth or illusion. This is the last choice, and if you choose truth, you will serve life, and if you choose illusion, you will rule life, so choose wisely. When we are moved by external forces, we can become an agent of creation or destruction, and history is full of instances where people and whole nations have been moved destructively. Water is matter, but waves, vortexes, currents, and fathomless depths are not matter. They are movements in matter. They are the property of energy. When we talk about energy, we often talk about how much energy a thing has or holds, but just as the waves in water is movement, so is energy in an object.

When we measure energy content in an object, we are measuring the potential energy movement in it. And how easy it is to move the atoms in that object. Since matter and energy are the same things and atoms or combinations of atoms are movement, energy is movement. High and low, left and right, hot and cold, rest and movement. These four directional units of measure are used as a reference point for matter. If one object of matter is one unit warmer than another object of matter, we say that the first object is hotter than the second object. We could more truthfully say that in the first object, the energy is moving faster, creating heat, than in the second object, but we need to use matter to measure the energy content and how it moves. To conserve matter and energy, one must know what action one will perform. Energy-effective beings only do what they intend, with no extra action or mistakes.

For them, all goes according to plan, and the plan is the best way to perform the intended action, so they consume exactly the amount of energy needed to perform the action. In water, the hydrogen wants to react to the change in energy, but the oxygen acts as a dampener preventing or restricting the hydrogen from reacting. There is often a small local reaction, often in the form of heat and/or kinetic energy in the form of waves. If the body of water is great, energy changes take time, or the change in energy must be big. If the body of water is small, it is easier for the hydrogen to react to the energy change. But there is a certain instance where oxygen does not restrict the movement of hydrogen as much. When water is at its anomaly point of +4 degrees Celsius, the bond between hydrogen and oxygen is at its weakest, but the density is at its highest, and we can use this to our advantage.

At +4 degrees, if we did not heat or cool the water but inferred energy kinetically raising the temperature slightly, the energy output would be greater than the input. The energy output would be greater if we could move it to the boiling point without heat. Water is the key we need in our quest. Water unlocks the energy needed to create things without heat. It is this faculty that we must use. If we used a process that uses and produces heat, we would need the energy of several planets to create what can be created. Water absorbs heat. In fact, it absorbs all kinds of energy, and when we combine it with a process that does not produce heat, we can maximise the energy output in the energy-rich hydrogen. Water is empty. It is, in a way, devoid of substance and direction. It is like a womb. It is ready to receive life and facilitate its growth.

As the food we eat becomes a part of us, when water enters a vessel, the energy signature of that vessel can either degrade the water's energy or the energy remains neutral. This is the best-case scenario, but in extremely rare cases, the vessel's energy can enhance water's energy. In this extreme case, the vessel has a higher energy signature than water without creating thermal energy.

Chapter 19

The plants and trees on this planet make more water than they consume. The smaller plants, flowers, and so on do not make water like the bigger plants. The Master of Water making are the leaf-growing trees and ferns. Some plants use more water than they consume, and that is because of their role in the system. Mushrooms are one of these 'plants' (fungi). The reason for this is their composition and role in the system as a facilitator of an information network between all living things in the system. Mushrooms need the energy that water holds to perform their function and use water as an amplifier and communication medium to do this. Mushrooms do not grow by themselves but in conjunction with a host of other plants and trees. They must be in a community for it to grow since it must have someone to communicate with, right?

Trees make sure that the temperature on the soil is low so that the water table does not retreat to deeper levels, hot soil is a barrier for water, and the shade keeps the rainwater on or close to the surface, making sure that all vegetation gets its fill of water under the protective branches of a tree. Trees are the parents of the forest. If the trees are healthy, then the rest of the forest will be healthy, but if the trees fall, the entire system will fall. If a forest has poor diversity or monoculture of trees, the trees, and the forest will slowly die. Without trees, the world becomes a desert. Trees use carbon dioxide and sunshine to create water and carbohydrates. Trees and plants can convert sunshine into hydrogen or, more correctly, to revert sunshine and light back into its original state, hydrogen. Plants and trees can, in various degrees, also convert and combine sunshine, hydrogen, carbon dioxide, and oxygen into sugar, fat, or water. In general, they create more of one and less of the other two.

How do trees and their function or ability to create fat, sugar, and water affect our quest? We can see a connection between the way we think trees support themselves and what they produce and what people need and produce. They say that we need money, but we produce money. They say we produce garbage, but in fact, we produce ideas and life. We do not need money since we produce it with our bodies or minds. If one makes a lot of money in this system, it only tells us that the system appreciates one's idea, mind, or body. And that it works well in the system. Nothing else, nothing that works against the system, would or could be successful. There are three types of people: those who create sugar, those who create fat, and those who create water. As with other living things, we create little of each, but our main activity should be one of these. Some exceptional people that are in contact with their higher being and source will have two or even all three of them. Leonardo da Vinci was one of them, and there are many more.

Those who produce sugar make life sweet and they are such people as artists, music makers, dancers, actors, painters, writers, etc. Those who produce fat make things for the physical world: architects, inventors, builders, carpenters, engineers, etc. Those who produce water are the trailblazers of development: philosophers, thinkers, scientists, and visionaries, people who create ideas, new thoughts, and new ways of looking at life and the human experience. Whichever way we choose to create it will increase our freedom and our abundance. If we create from truth and if we dare take a stand for what we love to do, what our hearts and soul need to do to feel happy, content, and free, the universe will not deny you. When we do things, we love doing, we feel free, and that is why we do them as often as we can. When we feel free, we feel like a million dollars. We feel wealthy and living in abundance. This is the nature of freedom. It makes you feel carefree, happy, and one with the forces of the universe. Like all the adventures waiting for you around the corner, it makes you feel like a child, so why would you want to feel differently in your life?

We who walk this path must act like trees: we must shelter, nourish, and support all living things around us. Be loving to those who climb our branches and see how our fruit will grow into new trees. Our bodies are of matter, and matter is energy, but matter cannot generate energy. Only the movement in matter can. The brain is matter.

Thoughts are not matter, they are waves in matter, but if this is so, what about consciousness? Is consciousness a movement in matter? First, we must ask the question, what is energy, and where did it come from? Matter is frozen energy, so it only holds potential energy. When moved or heated, it generates energy. When in rest nothing, so can energy only be generated when matter is moved or heated, or can energy be generated or exist without matter? At the beginning of our universe before the big bang, could there have been matter present? If so, where did it come from? Was it the remains of an earlier universe?

How much matter was it so that it could generate enough energy to create all matter in our universe? How and why did it move? There must be movement in matter to generate energy, remember? If it was the remains of an older universe, the energy in that universe would not be moving since the older universe must have been almost cold. There cannot have been a lot of moving matter or energy left? We must talk a little bit about energy and atoms before this question can be answered properly. Atoms connect or create bonds to form substances. Atoms vibrate so does the substance. We might not see it, but they do. Movement, in turn, creates heat; with faster movement, the heat increases, which in turn means more energy. Movement-heat-energy or movement = energy, so what is cold, non-movement, rest, nonenergy? Why do we not say anti-energy, and what is anti-energy? Nonenergy is better than anti-energy since everything is energy. Can anything then be anti-energy? The word 'anti' means against or in opposition to, which implies that anti-energy would be in opposition to energy. But if everything is energy, it would be in opposition to itself, a contradiction that creates some problems for us. Can something be created that is in total opposition to itself, can anti-energy or anti-matter exist. I do not think so it could just be sloppy wording.

Energy = matter = movement = heat = light = dynamic.

Nonenergy = matter = rest = cold = darkness = static. Energy and nonenergy are both made up of matter. When energy is released, there is movement and heat. When we burn coal, for instance, the lump of coal disintegrates, releasing heat, soot, light, and 'free' carbon atoms. Because it is not the carbon atoms that disintegrate but the bindings between the atoms, it is these bindings that create the physical lump of coal. The 'free' atoms that float away slow down, cooling and releasing less light. This is "spent" energy but not nonenergy. When a universe cools down, this means that all the energy is spent and that all connections are severed. All matter that the spherical universe began with is still there, but there are no longer any clusters of atoms that are bound to each other. All atoms are 'free'. The free atoms stay free because of the cold, so the free atoms cannot bind to each other. The cold and slow movement cannot generate enough energy to create bonds so that clusters of atoms can create matter so that there can be energy.

If a spherical universe is cold, 'dead', how did a new one rise in its place? Enter black holes? Black holes and, specifically, a super black hole in the middle of the universe, transport matter and light from the earlier universe to the becoming universe. Black holes regenerate matter by the gravitational pull that generates very high velocities, extreme cold, and pressure. Free atoms are pulled into the black hole at a velocity that is close to the speed of light. The cold and pressure in the black hole compress these atoms into raw energy. Under these conditions it forms a sea of energy that is in a state of equilibrium in the black hole. If and I think there are enough black holes in this universe to suck up all the spent energy, matter. To create larger black holes that will eat smaller black holes until there is one super black hole that contains all matter in the universe. That super black hole is the egg of the universe, and the matter is the sperm. The super black hole will pull everything towards itself at speeds that will be close to the speed of light. All matter and smaller black holes in the universe will be pulled towards it, and as everything comes crashing into this super black hole, it will explode, throwing all matter into a new sphere and creating the foundation for a new universe.

This is how a universe comes and goes into being. There is as much energy in the preceding as in the succeeding universe. The first law of thermodynamics states that energy cannot be destroyed or created. In this super black hole, for a split second that lasts an eternity, all energy is united and connected. In that black hole, all matter is in a state of total equilibrium. Nothing can move, but there is movement, heat but absolute freezing, light but pitch dark, where everything is and is not. This is where creation happens. This is the point of our origin where all consciousness was formed. Our consciousness is this energy field in our bodies, and it energises us in our sleep during the dream period when the consciousness connects to the field. During sleep, our minds try to control our dreams to do what the mind does best, and that is to analyse and solve 'problems'. When we dream, the mind tries to solve a problem or problems in the material world. What ends up happening often is a confused, sometimes unintelligible set of short films that play out in our dreams that do not seem to have any connections, but somehow, they connect. I believe that this is the result of our connection to this energy field with our consciousness.

When our consciousness connects with the energy field, the field that holds all energy and all possibility, it is home, but the mind is in deep waters. The consciousness and the energy field are the same. The previous is a drop of water, and the latter is the ocean. The drop understands that there are endless possibilities that can manifest in the universe in any scenario. The mind cannot manage endlessness. It needs a few possible outcomes. Because the physical world is limited, and so is the mind. This limitation has formed the mind, and it works well within its boundaries. A novel idea comes from the consciousness, not the mind. The mind cannot manage ideas or concepts that transcend the limits that the mind has staked out for itself. Only the consciousness can move or break down those boundaries. The mind tends to become fearful when it finds itself in uncharted territory. It is scared and believes its modus operandi will not be useful in navigating this unfamiliar territory because it cannot predict any familiar outcome, good or bad. Consciousness is the movement in matter, and the mind is the matter. This drop of endless energy siphons energy to our bodies and minds from the energy field, and we collectively energise the whole earth and the universe as all other living beings in this universe do.

The sentient being's mind is the most powerful and weakest of all minds because of our free will. We can choose to listen to our consciousness or not, so we are pivotal to the energy and possibility that can manifest in the physical universe. If we harmonise with the source energy field, then we will replenish energy in the world and universe as well as introduce all kinds of possibilities to it. But if we choose not to listen, energy will replenish slowly, and only the possibility we can predict or make sense of, the mind will manifest. A mind that does not listen to its consciousness will be disturbed, and its logic will only follow the physical world's logic, even if it is incorrect and harmful. It will not replenish the universe. It will take energy and create heat, speeding towards destruction, hoping, and thinking it is on its way to heaven. We can see this in our minds, nothing or no one is truly holy everyone is disposable. We do not care about life or freedom except for ourselves. The greater the distance from consciousness and source, the more chaos and chance we experience in our lives. You cannot be in a state of harmony if you experience chaos or lucky encounters in any field of your life. But regardless of that, you experience the true state of the universe as an inharmonious harmony.

The universe will always be right regardless of what happens to us because of free will, and consciousness is the failsafe to free will. Free will is for the mind so that one can truly experience consciousness. Source and life have a purpose for us, and I think that it will not let us go before we experience that purpose. Even if we must live through many universes and lives to reach it. In our individual lives, we need to find and conduct our purpose because every one of us is a piece of the puzzle, and all the pieces matter, so you and the choices you make matter. If you do not find and conduct your purpose, you are essentially wasting your life. If we must fulfil our material and spiritual purpose, what is the reason for this? If all energy that we and all things in the universe, including the universe, comes from source or the energy field, then why do we not fulfil our purpose from there? Why has source made it hard for us? There must be a good and valid reason for this. Why do we have to work on our purpose from here in the flesh, matter with amnesia, and what are we individually and collectively supposed to achieve that would warrant us to come here?

This book is about matter, and at the end of this book, we will know what it is, how it behaves, and what we are supposed to do with it. When we are here, we are immersed in matter, and it seems that we are supposed to free ourselves from it. That does not actually make a lot of sense. Why did we come here in matter from spirit, energy, source, whatever you want to call it, to free ourselves from matter? Why would the universe take us from a place where we are not bound in matter to a place where we will be bound in matter? The whole idea seems to free yourself from matter and return to where you were free of matter. No, this makes no sense, and it seems to be an exercise in futility. I think that the road to our purpose goes through matter, not around it. Matter is energy, just as we are energy and consciousness, and it is this energy that animates matter and our bodies. We are connected to this energy, throughout the universe. We need to awaken our consciousness and make sure that our mind permanently takes a backseat from that point on. When we let the mind rule, and it is a terrible master, we suffer immensely. Being in mind and ignoring consciousness will increase suffering in you and the world.

When the mind cannot predict an outcome due to a lack of information or too many variables, it gets frightened and starts to envision bad scenarios. This is a consequence of its limited beliefs and not being connected to source energy. It is also a survival strategy to make the body ready for fight or flight, a warning signal to 'get ready'. The mind raises the alarm to its silent master, the consciousness. *Please take over, I am afraid.* And when the consciousness takes over, it can manifest as calmness or intuition if we pay attention to it. When this happens on a large scale in a group or population, the mind raises the alarm that it cannot predict the future outcome. If no one is listening to the collective consciousness, then it tends to escalate into situations that deteriorate rapidly into the bad experiences that the limited mind envisions and creates. The mind tries to control its fear by creating outcomes it thinks will reduce the fear and predicts a 'good' future, and how do we normally reduce the fear? We attack it, kill it. The mind tries to connect to the collective consciousness, but we can only do that if we are asleep or are connected to our consciousness. Since we are not, we go into a spiral of fear and violence.

Chapter 20

So how do we wake up? Well, we need a lot of people who are conscious so that they can tip the balance. Or we need a person so connected to the collective consciousness and source that he/she can function as a conduit for people to connect to their consciousness. What these highly spiritual people do is, with a loud and clear voice, say: *Wake up, this is not real.* Many of us will wake from the nightmare and envision another way of dealing with our fear, but if none of these two options happens, we will have to live out the nightmare. This is the reason we must pay attention to ourselves and know that we are not the mind. You are the consciousness that sees and hears the mind. Only by doing this can one take responsibility for one's actions and life. This is how we get out of the cycle of fear and suffering.

How do we awaken the consciousness within, meditation, psychedelics, controlling the mind, and body, no sex, no sleep, no food, reading or listening to masters telling us how they did it? They can help, but these methods are not the answer. If they were, there would be many more people totally connected to the collective consciousness than we see today or during any period in time. There must be a way for us to 'become' conscious without all the pain and hardships which does not take years of effort to reach. There is, but first, we must be ready to be awakened. People, in general, do not rely on, trust, or dare to take responsibility for their lives or to become liberated beings. Apparently, we are having too much fun. Prison is safer and more comfortable than freedom since freedom means you must love the truth and be responsible for your actions and all their ripple effects.

To gain this freedom, one must die. You must 'kill' the mind and hurl that matter from the cliffs into the water so that you can go back into spirit and become a free being. This has been done many times during humanity's walk to free itself. It is not enough if you do not fear death and bravely try to gain freedom. It will not be enough if you fear death but still think it is worth trying to reach freedom. What you truly fear is love, truth, responsibility, and your purpose. Living a life where you are totally connected to source, yourself, and every decision you make is in the light of truth and love. There is no vacation from this life. Nowhere you can hide and be 'human' for a short while. You must give up your mind, and all that the mind wants. Prison sounds nicer, doesn't it? Becoming an awakened being is not a glamorous calling. On the contrary, all responsibility and no rewards since you are doing natural source work which is our natural work. You do not get rewarded for what you should be doing.

By surrendering oneself to source, one must do the work of source in the physical world according to one's purpose: this is your path. You will end up loving doing it, but you might not have any personal goals to fulfil. Everything the mind wants to achieve, reach, do, or experience will be discarded for the work of source and your purpose. There will be no excuses. You will never again be the mind with small needs and preferences to play with. So now that we know what is demanded of us, how do we become what we used to be? First, we become healers so that you will know how to manipulate matter. As a healer, you should begin by healing yourself, and as a healer, we will enhance our respect for life and humanity. You will know how and why we suffer when we do not listen to our heart or consciousness. We must first love ourselves and life and be responsible before we become powerful. And then, we can begin reshaping matter and energy. Healing is the reshaping of cells (matter), that have become damaged by too much or too little energy flowing to the part that requires healing. When people get sick, we must look at least two points. If a part gets too much energy, then another part is not getting enough, the system is not balanced. One part is overloading, another is starving, and as a healer, you must understand how energy works regardless of the system because that is what healers do. Healers correct energy flows in systems.

By healing yourself, you heal the people around you and the world. First, we heal then we create. Without self-healing, there will not be self-love. Without self-love, there will be no love. Without love, there will be no truth. Without truth, there will be no peace. Without peace, there will only be suffering. We start by listening to the heart, hearing and feeling it pounding in your chest, feeling how it flows energy to all parts of your body, healing, cleansing, forgiving, and comforting all past wrongdoings and pains. Begin with healing the heart, then move on to the part or parts you know need healing until you have healed yourself completely. Feel how the warm, loving energy flows from your heart and around your heart, healing and energising it so that the heart can be free in love and truth. This is female and male energy. Love is female, and truth is male, soft and hard, dark and light, embracing and penetrating. One cannot heal without love and truth. Most of us cannot understand the concept of love. Love and truth are not separated. They are one, both penetrating and embracing. When you genuinely love someone or something, you do not only feel caring, compassion, and so on but the truth about your connections to the object. You want them to become the best version of themselves because you want to be the best version of yourself regardless of your connection to the other.

Do not try to bring out the best version of someone else or you will create dependency with that person, and they will grow to resent you for it. This means that both of you are trapped in a relationship where your happiness is dependent on the other person, and if they falter, you will feel bad. You will blame them for making you feel less than the best. One can do or say things that will make people feel that one loves them but try to tell them the truth about yourself and, in so doing, the truth about them, and I will guarantee you most people will not feel loved by you anymore. Because so many of us do not live in truth, we really hate it when someone sees what we already know but try so hard to hide. An exercise to heal oneself is breathing and doing it that matches your internal rhythm. OM breathing is one way to understand healing and creation. Begin by inhaling, followed by exhaling Ooo, Mmm. You divide the exhalation into three parts. The first two parts sound like an Ooo or Aaa, Uuu, and the last part is a Mmm before you need to inhale. When used as an exercise, the word OM (Aum) encompasses the universe and creation. In the first part, the word comes from the deep and the left and travels to the right. In the second part, the word comes from the right and travels to the centre. The third part comes from the centre and travels in and to the deep.

The word *Aum* is a circle, a cycle where death and birth is a point on the circle. Life is what happens when we travel from the point back to the point of creation, being, and death. The circle is curved so that one cannot look forward or backward in a straight line to see the future or the past. One can only see the moment, be here, and now in the point where you are standing; everything else is out of sight. We will come back to the word *Aum* in the third book and its usage of it in the final stage of our investigation. The word is how source creates the universe. The first exhale (Aaa) is a sigh of joy, relief, and release of energy, and everything comes into being. Then the second word (Uuu), all of creation is coming into place and maturing, and then the final word (Mmm), everything is falling apart, death. Death and rebirth are joined in the exhale. Death is where everything is blown out. There is a point where the exhale turns and becomes an inhale. This is death and rebirth in one motion. This is what our universe is. This simple breath no more, no less, as above so below.

When using the *Aum* chanting or meditation, you must feel the A-U-M. Feel each letter. Are they in harmony in your throat? Do they vibrate in harmony with each other, do not force them as I did in the beginning. My A's were off and hard as I was trying to force creation, but over time, I could sense the issue. I knew what it meant. I wanted so desperately to create a new reality for myself that I was trying to force and push my A's out so that I could rest in my U's and die in my M's. The A's were off; the U's were better, and the M's were best, but the *Aum* was off, and I had to heal my fears and impatience before I could enjoy *Aum*. The harmony within the word will create harmony within you and your life. When you chant, it can bring you peace and clarity if you get the right vibration.

If we look closely, we can see it all around us in nature. It is nature. In our movements and our thoughts and ideas in all our activities, look even closer, and you will see how that circle gives birth to new circles. These circles form patterns revealing shapes or networks, an imprint of creation. They are all connected to each other, and when the first one collapses, they all collapse, leaving an empty space with infinite possibilities until it begins again. For me, at least, there is extraordinary beauty in this to be a part of this breath, and it is reassuring knowing that it all will begin again. All this wonder and joy, this calm dedication to life and no matter what happens to me. Or what people do to each other, or nature, it will begin anew somewhere sometime. There is no fear in creation, but many of us fear physical death. To fear death is to fear birth. This is illogical and tells us how far we are from nature. When we fear death, we try to separate ourselves from this breath, the natural order of life, which is unhealthy. This separation leads us to live broken, fragmented lives where we are waging war on our whole existence, causing pain and suffering to everything we touch.

Our great-grandchildren are calling us from the edge of time and creation, watching the exhale becoming an inhale. And in awe seeing the death of this universe and its timeline with the knowledge that it all will begin again. We must deliver them, thereby living lives that will take us to that point in time where we can look upon death and know, truly know that it is the rebirth we are seeing.

The transmutation of energy needs to be learnt and mastered when we heal. We do it all the time food goes in and turns into energy you can use for any activity. We do it unconsciously with food, but we need to do it so we can learn to do it consciously with breathing or other functions. For instance, next time you are tired, you energise yourself with food, music, or whatever you choose to, see if you can control where the energy goes. Let us get into the transmutation of energy and when we can control and

129

direct where and how much energy a part or activity will get or use. We can then more effectively heal ourselves and others. Both healing and transmutation of energy are natural to us, although we tend not to think that it is so. It is impossible to heal or transmute energy when you are in a state of fear. We can only think of ourselves or loved ones when we feel fear. To do healing and transmutation well, one must have conscious focus, clear intention, and love. A big bonus is if the object being healed also is in those mental states, so that the body is ready and willing to receive the healing, cooperating, so to speak.

The body is a temple, but it is form and perishable, and the consciousness is formless form and indestructible. When we let our mind be led or guided by consciousness, we can understand that sickness, pain, and death is no different from health, joy, and life on the level of consciousness. The latter is just an expression of an unbalanced energy state in the system. To be able to do healing, the healer's energy flow must be optimal, and to reach optimal flow, you must heal yourself first. If we do not heal ourselves first, we are charlatans who do not understand life, death, health, or sickness. Moreover, we cannot ensure lasting change within and around us in the physical world. When we heal, it is a co-creation between your consciousness and your body and someone else consciousness. When the healer's consciousness connects with the subject, they share knowledge about the energy field that the healer and subject share. The healer's work is to direct energy to the part or parts that need to be healed.

The healer uses his or her energy to guide the subject's energy to remove blockages or increase flow to the affected parts. They now work together to heal the subject. We can look at the subject as a novice healer, not an object to be operated on. You must do it together for the best result.

Chapter 21

A healer must be in harmony within herself so that she can bring harmony into the 'patient', and in so doing, work together to heal the patient. The healer must also be in touch with her consciousness and let it guide and reveal what is wrong with the patient. Many healers do this intuitively already. If you are new to healing, do not listen to your mind. It will mess things up. The mind is separate from consciousness and nature and cannot manage this situation, with too many variables. Healing and transmutation of energy, all of this has to do with matter. We can only transmute energy in matter, not in the energy field. Energy cannot hurt or heal energy, but it can hurt or heal the vessel energy is in. This is about how we take care of matter with energy; we can use energy to heal or hurt, but can we use energy to create or destroy matter? We know the answer to this question, yes, but matter is energy, and energy cannot be destroyed or created. A better formulation is that it can be dissolved or gathered, integrated to flow in harmony. We see this in nature around us all the time, so if we can see it, why can we not do it? If we can learn to heal and transmute, can we learn to create? The creation of matter can and should be as natural as healing since they both work and operate on the same principle. In healing, you direct energy to a part so that it can have a better energy flow. By directing energy, you are in the learning phase, you are controlling energy, and energy is movement in matter.

When learning this ability, it is easy to think that one is special and being a kind of Superman banishing the wicked and helping the good, (and helpless). This is, of course, very wrong, so stop that (I have had these fantasies as well). There are no good (helpless) or bad (action-oriented) people. There are whole and separated people. Separated people do not win in the long run since they do not recognise wholeness as the fundamental state of the universe. You cannot divide that which is indivisible. Anyone who proclaims someone else as being at fault is separating themselves or others from the whole and, in so doing, becomes a part of the problem. Therefore, healers are so important for us and the world now. For far too long, we have been living lives in cultures that believe that separation between people, God, and nature is natural, not understanding that this notion is the root cause of our suffering. This separation has created suffering in our personal lives, but this is also why we, as a collective, suffer so badly at our own hands. Separation is cancer, as one part of the organism demands more resources than it needs to function optimal. This can hurt or even kill an organism. This sickness is the root of all sicknesses.

The healer cooperates in healing with the patient, and what they are doing is breaking the shackles of separation.

The healer imparts his or her wisdom to the patient about healing and that they together are going to heal the patient. The healer cannot, in fact, heal the patient without his or her knowledge and engagement. The healer is a guide, guiding her energy and the attention and the energy of the patient to the part that needs to be healed. This frees the shackles of bondage since the healer is not the pivotal power in the healing process. All the power of healing and decision-making is in the hands of the patient, not the healer. When healing this way, every patient is treated as a novice before the session and as a master afterward. In that way, every session creates a new healer, and this is what can save us since who does not want to be healed and healthy? The master healer teaches the novice to use her 'forgotten' healing power. This is the only way I know how to change, how we perceive ourselves and the world. By guiding people to a small part of their inner light and letting them explore and understand the rest for themselves.

Healing people this way is not claiming authority over anyone. This is, in my eyes, the only way to heal people and the world. Consciousness knows that it only has the authority of itself and can never hold it over any other consciousness. When working with our consciousness, we are in a state of mind where we are not exerting force on anyone. To be a powerful healer and guide, a healer must be in this state of mind. The universe does not require healing but we as humans do. Man has strayed far from nature and the natural ways of humans and the universe.

Healing must be done by humans as a collective so that we can find our way back to nature and live in more harmony. Collective healing will make us move forward with more intentions of what we as a species want to achieve. Our lives are lived in cultures that deny our natural born freedom. The purpose of this might be to shape us into productive citizens, where we are both prisoners and jailers. Instead of seeing fault in our shared culture that we create together, we see fault in others and ourselves.

When seeing fault in others, we shift fear, anger, and the feeling of inability to change our situation to someone outside of our tribe or family. Those other people seem to be causing the situation, forcing me to react in a negative, violent way, so everything is their fault. But if I instead blame myself for the situation without the knowledge that I can change the whole setup of me and the situation. I will just see that my inability to change and the ability to attract negative situations, are equally high and that I cannot better myself. It seems that my life the way I am living it, only make things worse. Both types of people will create calamity and suffering in their communities; the latter will be actively violent, and the former will be passively violent. However, both will tear apart their community in time. In being a healer, you are also a warrior who can see the cold hard truth and decide what to do in a given situation. Even if it means taking a life. The better you become as a healer, the better you will become at seeing the truth and knowing when to end life. The difference between healing and killing is essentially none. One creates paths, and the other closes paths, two sides of the same coin.

Life and death are inseparable, and preferring one always puts you in direct opposition to existence and creates suffering in life. An interesting question arises, can one kill a person who is deeply connected to source before his or her time? We need people that are females, males, healers, warriors, inactive, active, receiving and transmitting. We need people who can be both. We already have a whole planet full of people who are separated from the nature of humanity by being one or the other. And in the worst cases neither, people need to become whole. If we as a species want to make it to the stars, we need to be whole. We cannot enter the universe fractured. We will only bring our petty conflicts to the universe. I know that every human being has the capability to become whole, but many will lack willpower and the discipline and even the knowledge to make an effort, so those who can do it will help others. We cannot create a divide between these two groups. Those who become whole must guide and protect those who are healing so that they can evolve in their own time. Those who do not evolve are not given the opportunity to hurt others physically or mentally.

These restrictions are precarious because they can lead to oppression, 'the road to hell is lined with good intentions." Seemingly conscious people will become oppressive given the right circumstance. When we are here in matter, we must do our best to create a world that is built on love, truth, and freedom. If we do this for ourselves and others, this worldly life will be filled with joy and evolution. We will reach the highest pinnacle that humans can reach with a minimum of suffering and pain. For healers and warriors, the healing part is love, feminine, and enclosing, and the warrior part is truth, masculine, and penetrating. The former is soft, and the latter is hard. All of us must strive to be both. Love and truth, feminine and masculine, soft and hard. If you do this, the sky is the limit, and pain and suffering will be reduced. Begin your training with love and healing because when you face the truth later, you will not become hard since love and your heart were developed first and are more evolved. Many men are taught to be hard before being taught to be loving, and vice versa is the case for women. Why are we surprised that men and women do not connect properly?

When we make ourselves whole, we heal a part of the universe, a part of humanity, and it prepares us and the universe for the next stage of evolution. The more people that become whole, the closer we come to the tipping point for change, but the opposite is also true. When more people get separated, we reach the opposite tipping point where we get further away from change and deeper into the material world. The change will always be around the corner. The only question is, are you ready to embrace it, or are you going to run screaming from it? You can only suffer more by running. Change often presents itself when we experience more pain than joy in our system. Resistance often stems from ignorance of what is happening. This ignorance results in fear, making us fearful of the change that our consciousness knows must occur for the suffering and pain to stop. The fearful mind only sees bad outcomes and wrongly predicts that it will be worse after the change because the future is uncharted.

When you can incorporate truth about what is going on in life with the love of yourself. Not becoming fearful of the change that is coming, you will not resist it. Some people believe that 'powerful people' are trying to direct the change to a place of their choosing, and this might be right. That can only be done when we are separated within ourselves and having a fearful mind. Then the people can be guided wherever the puppet masters wish us to go: "Just follow the yellow brick road." If we are whole, no one can make us fearful. With love and truth, we will see through the deception. When whole, we will let the change occur naturally unopposed, but it might still be painful because we needed it in the first place. The change will not hurt more than it needs to, and we will know that the change will be necessary for our evolution. When healing or transmuting energy, you must acknowledge the truth about what you are doing, and you cannot lie. You do need love, but you must have truth. Love will save energy because love for the patient will make your part easier. Truth will keep your consciousness sharp on why you are doing it and make you ready to take the consequence if anything goes wrong.

People who use force or deception are wizards, and those who use co-creation are mages. This is a general description of two different ways to transmute energy.

There is a third way, but we must wait for book 3 for that. When we want to create, there is a limitation we must consider, and that is consciousness. When your consciousness is on board with what you want to create, the time factor can sometimes be eliminated. When you go against your consciousness, the time it takes to create something is endless. One can say that it is a scale. The further away you are from your consciousness, the more time it takes, and vice versa. This is one reason you must become a healer first so that you align with your heart and consciousness before you become hard with truth. Truth does not corrupt, but it will make you cold and hard and can make you forget that it will hurt people who are not ready for the truth. Why do we make ourselves suffer? Why don't we live the lives we believe we want and need, to be the best person we can be? Why are we holding on to our own suffering? What is the purpose of this? How does it serve us? Is it just old programming that runs in the background of our minds? Why did we install it, and can it be removed?

Most of the time, my own suffering is torturing me, and I do not want it to go on, but still, it seems that I cannot let it go since I am still in it. I cannot move past it to the empty space where I can be free. Freedom is what I want for all the people of the world and for myself: the choice to choose what our hearts desire without hurting anyone. I cannot accept that anyone would have to suffer for my choice. Otherwise, I might have to suffer for someone else's choice. My suffering, and probably everyone's suffering that is self-induced, comes from the uncomfortable truth that what I think I need and want is not in connection with my consciousness and heart. What I want is not what I truly want and need for the path I will walk. When we measure time, we measure when and how much matter has changed. There seems to be no time outside of the physical realm. But matter is energy, and energy is movement, so is the movement in matter, time? Yes, when that energy is bound in matter. Otherwise, it is timeless. When we dream or meditate, or have visions, there is no time. What signifies time is when we deal with the mind (matter) and the body. In consciousness, there is no time. I can traverse a million years in a second, so in these states where time does not exist, how do we let our consciousness override the mind and its belief in time?

We are made of matter, and we live in a world made of matter. This is undeniable. We interact with matter every day, but behind all matter, there is an emptiness where matter is not frozen energy but just energy. In that space where energy flows and rocks slowly like an ocean. Energy can flow in any direction, and here every possible and impossible outcome exists. In this space, we can, with our consciousness, direct energy to flow to where it needs to be for an event or object to manifest. The mind abhors timelessness. It cannot stand it because, without time, there is no point of reference. A point of reference is static, but it has no anchor in timelessness. Everything is fluid like an ocean, always shifting into the next thing. The small mind cannot grasp that. It cannot form a cohesive 'reality'. It has no ground to stand on. The mind should only be used for running the day-to-day task of the material world, physical activities, and calculations. This makes me believe that we do not dare let go of the mind as the chief operator of our lives when it only should be the technical operator of our bodies. Our minds are horrible jailers, but it is my jailer, and every other mind seems to be worse than mine. I do not really have any experience that I trust, or that lasted long enough to release me from its bond. If I stopped letting the mind run the show, it would free me from the tyranny of the mind and time. The real question is, do we really want to be free? To take that leap of faith to become an entity that has no bonds, free of all constraints, free to be and do whatever our hearts desire. To reach into the core of ourselves and the universe and look upon the truth of everything.

Because if we do this, we will no longer be a person or a name that has a timeline, a set past, or a future. We will no longer have a fixed family or friends. We will no longer have a fixed point of reference to bind us to a place in space and time. We will have the choice to be where we want or need to be. Matter is important to us as we choose to hold it as our master and slave. It rules us, but we rule it as well, and we cannot ignore it when we are in our corporeal form, but it should not be our master or slave. It should be a trusted friend. Nature and the nature of matter are the same, being as they are inseparable from each other. When we understand this, we can see the connections that they form within us and how inseparable we are from nature, and how its law is our law. If we do not obey that law, death will come like a thief in the night, but when we obey the law, physical death will be a choice we make. Just to be clear, immortality in a physical body cannot be achieved, nor should you wish or desire it. We must consider the nonphysical part of life regarding immortality, dreams, memories, fantasies, and experiences will probably entangle if you would live 1000, 10,000 or 100 000 years. The mind does not handle time well. As discussed earlier, one would probably become an incoherent person that has forgotten its point of reference in time.

Chapter 22

To be free, absolutely free, you must be absolutely responsible for all your actions. There is no one or nothing you can blame for your victories or failures. There is only you, and we have a problem with this notion. This is the reason we seek authority outside of us for guidance and to take charge of our lives and actions. We dare not be responsible for our own lives because we do not believe in a benevolent universe where dreams can come true. Freedom is responsible for all your actions and your children (consequences). Are we ready for that? Do most of us dare to be completely responsible for our thoughts, speech, and physical actions? To liberate oneself is not very hard. All you have to do is to be consistent, so it is the hardest thing you can do. Just stop listening to your mind. Your mind should be used for simple problem-solving, bodily functions, and all the mundane chores in your daily life. Begin with listening to your consciousness when riding the bus, subway, or car. Be present and try to focus on that empty space where the mind becomes quiet.

Our minds are problem solvers from the ancient past and have a hard time coping with today's cultures and societies. The mind cannot see the difference between a lion in a bush, or a deadline for a job and the possibility of being fired if missed. It will react in the same way: fight, flight, or freeze. We are using a mind that reacts to every stimulus so it can spot the lion. But there are no more lions to spot, but a million other 'dangers' that society perceives as, social lions. The mind has a tough time not going overboard with the dangers that you must avoid, so your stress levels skyrocket. The mind is constantly chattering away about how you are navigating wrongly in this world. This is because it treats every little mistake as a, 'you are dead' moment because it only sees lions, not a fart in a full elevator. When we surrender ourselves to nature and the universe, we let it work its magic at its natural pace. When we develop with nature, we realise that we *are* nature and do not need to force ourselves or nature to do our will. This is hard to accept since we think we live such short lives, but a life that is lived following the nature of the universe is long and full of experiences and joy. Many of us believe that if we let go of our will and let nature take its course, nothing good will happen, and I will become a bum in the streets. I cannot trust that nature's universe will give me what I need and want.

When we surrender control of our bodies and start to listen to them and the natural phases of bodily functions, we will know what it needs to function properly. This fact is often overlooked. Most of us ignore what the body tries to tell us. We should listen more carefully to our consciousness, universe, and body. They are always talking to us, every second of our lives. They are telling us the truth about our body, our purpose, and the function of the universe and everything in it. Just listen. The truth about everything is always there to be remembered. All we must do is listen and observe and be open to what is being said and acted out. You did not long to be born, nor did you shy away from it. You came because you wanted to experience the physical body and the world, even for a moment in time. Your consciousness would have rejoiced with incredible joy if you had died ten seconds after being born just to have the delicious feeling of being in matter. It would have no regrets, or feelings of sorrow for the lack of experience, but only joy to know the feeling of a fading heartbeat.

So, we are here full of joy and gratefulness for still being here. Even if we usually do not let our mind recognise this state, we should not spend our time in anger or sorrow. Feelings will pass as our lives will pass, and do not fear death because you did not fear birth. Just enjoy the coming and going of events and experiences, relax, and do what you can to make your existence in this world pleasurable for all. When transmuting energy or healing, you use the energy in an object or part, to flow from one place to another. Redirecting energy from one part should be done with care, and purpose that benefit the whole. If you take from one part, another part might experience a shortage. The focus should be to balance the energy flow in systems and bodies to alleviate stress in those systems. If we use objects outside our body to transmute or infuse more energy into the body, be you should be careful. Your body can hold a lot of energy, but too much can be damaging.

There are two ways of doing this: force or cooperation. Force implies will and direction. Cooperation on the other hand, means that you find an object that wants to give its gift of energy to you and heal or create something. The latter holds more power. Power is always stronger when we cooperate. When we force something, it will never be as strong as cooperation based on free will. We see this fact all around us: a community of people can be immensely stronger than a government, the American War of Independence, for example. To be in harmony with the nature of the universe, we use cooperation: a complete trust that what is good for the universe is good for me. We flow with the universe and our consciousness. Let's try some healing, transmuting of energy using yourself and objects. There are many ways to do this. Find one that works for you.

We can start by trying to transfer energy from the body to our hands. The goal is to make them warmer. Lie down and feel how your body is warm, and where energy runs through your it. Now start to draw energy from the main energy centre, the stomach. Direct it to your hands and feel how they get warmer. If it does not work, try again later but continue until you succeed in warming your hands. Do this as many times as you can until you can do it whenever you like, and it works. Listen to your body, how it responds: Does it hurt somewhere? Let us try some healing and draw energy from ourselves, the universe, the sun, or anything we feel you can draw energy from. Direct the energy to the place you need or want to heal, feel that part becoming warmer, and do this until you feel it is enough. When you know how to direct, heal, and transmute energy to yourself, then you can try on someone who is willing, and remember to begin small. Once again, draw energy from outside of yourself and direct it down into the patient and the part that needs healing, checking if it feels good and warm, and remembering cooperation is the key. You and the person must be in a relaxed state with each other, going over the body and finding the places that are receiving too little or too much energy. Then you begin by redirecting energy from the parts that get too much. Begin slowly and with small units of energy so that you do not create discomfort. Continue until the person feels that the pain has receded, then stop. You probably need to do this multiple times before it is completely healed and, in so doing, reset the system to its natural balance. The habitation of this 'new' balance needs to take hold, so make sure you keep on doing the healing until the new balance is natural.

The most important thing to do now is to give your knowledge to the person you have healed. Teach them how to heal themselves, how to become a healer. You must do this because every human can do this, so we must teach everyone who wants to know how to heal themselves and others. This is how we as a species evolve, by teaching each other how to realise our own ability and power to change ourselves into what we want to become. When you have learnt the art of transmuting, healing, cooperation, and teaching, you are on the way to transforming yourself to the natural state of being, a free human in every regard. The next step for us is to become a warrior. This entails, among other things using the word *no*. To things that do not serve you, nature, the universe, and things that will cause pain and suffering. How do you know what will cause pain and suffering? You have to listen with your heart and your consciousness. They will tell you what you need to know. This is the reason you must 'know thyself', and train yourself to recognise the right action and thoughts. All thoughts and actions have consequences, this is one reason why we start with healing. When an action is about to manifest like a drop of water on a blade of grass, its consequence is about to manifest as well. When we are healers, we are careful in our actions because we do not wish to inflict pain, now or later. A warrior only acts when he/she must, and only to prevent greater pain and suffering. In this position of strength, if a negative consequence arises, the warrior deals with it. Since the action taken was to reduce or prevent suffering, the warrior can expect resistance.

Remember, no action is action too, and sometimes it can be the best action. The heart and the consciousness know, leaving the mind to do its thing to run the bodily functions. Be the warrior that you are by practicing saying *no* to yourself and others. By knowing when you perform an action what the consequence will be, pain and suffering or healing and joy. Know thy self and where your limits lie, where you may go, and where you need to stop or retreat. Know thy self, and by knowing your limits, you will become limitless. Reject no one since the ocean rejects no water. That is why water is abundant and can form oceans. Cooperation is non opposition when we are in our hearts and consciousness, every day. Then you will be able to not oppose an idea or an action because you will flow with the universe, and it will be sanctioned by your heart and consciousness. It will lead to success regardless of if the outcome is 'good or bad'. When we cooperate with the universe, we do not second-guess it about the outcome. We just let it happen, trusting that the universe knows what needs to happen is right. This is how we become a master of ourselves. When your mind does not interfere and oppose your will, and what is about to happen.

The last thing you need to develop is the skill of the Hermit. The healer heals herself and the world. The healer considers consequences and avoids those who cause pain and suffering, and acts with heart and love. The warrior says *no* and acts to stop or prevent pain and suffering from escalating. The warrior expects consequences and deals with them as they arise and acts with heart and truth. The Hermit is the part of you that rests in the womb of the universe after an action has been performed. You will know that you need to rest when you have performed an action. It will feel natural. When we retreat into seclusion, we need to meditate on what has happened. We meditate on our action, and if it was the right action to take, especially at the beginning of this journey. We must rest in the universe and let it replenish us with energy and wisdom. Take a quiet moment from the world and all its people and the demands on us. No strong wind can blow all day. Go into yourself and examine what and how you have performed the action. Evaluate your intention for doing it and whether it was the right thing to do. This is an effective way to prevent yourself from becoming corrupt or dogmatic in your beliefs and actions. Do not become a slave to your beliefs. Let them stay sharp, and fluid like a river and not stale and putrid like a puddle. Many religious, political, and personal beliefs are stale. The reason for this is a false notion that if you hold fast to an idea, or belief, you are solid and show character.

In fact, you are showing weakness. The inability to change or incorporate new knowledge is a sign of a dead or dying system, be it a person, religion, political or cultural system. The river flows vigorously and replenishes itself because it does not reject the rain. So, it can replenish the ocean since the ocean does not reject the river. The Hermit is the final part you must play before you play the part of the healer or warrior. After a period of replenishment, you can act with energy and wisdom again to heal the world and find the truth about yourself and the universe. Beliefs, ideas, and convictions are dangerous because they tend to become stale and static. If they do, you will try hard to bend the world and people to your beliefs. This is the state of becoming an oppressor, not following the natural way of the universe, becoming corrupt, and controlling the outcome, so it fits your beliefs. Many people have done this with horrible results causing pain and suffering for themselves and others. If you want to be a Healer, Warrior, and Hermit, you must always be ready to rebel, abandon, and even betray all your ideas, beliefs, and convictions. You must be ready to rebel, abandon and even betray the universe and source. If this sounds wrong, or you refuse to even think that thought, you are not ready to become a Healer, Warrior, and Hermit. You are not ready to follow the Dao.

By being willing to abandon all that you know and hold as true, you are admitting to yourself and the universe that you know nothing, that all that you have learnt can, in fact be false. That these things are only figments of your mind and that you have seen truths where there are no truths, seen connections that do not actually connect. Only a wise person can admit to herself that all they have come to hold true, can and might, in fact, be wrong. Or that they do not know or see the whole picture. When you admit this to yourself, a sense of true freedom comes over you. In that space, you can rest and let the universe do its thing, and you will become a beacon, a conduit for the universe to act through, and with you. You and the universe will start to cooperate, co-creating to the will of the universe, which is you, and us, to naturally develop to its will to become what it must become. When you do this, the universe will reward you, but you will not want anything, only to serve the universe and life. So, that it can manifest the best version of itself and evolve to its final form. When we let things be, so that they can develop on their own. They will naturally follow the way of the universe and become the best they can be in that time and space. To be in matter, you must be in service to the energy in matter, the universe, and life. This is to be in service with matter but not trapped in matter. When you are in service, you have the mandate by the universe to change and create, so that all life can benefit from your creations. In this way, the universe can work through you to manifest itself in the world. This will be your purpose, your gift to the universe and yourself, to be a part of the nature of the universe. A conscious part of all that occurs in this universe in our time, and this will be a part of our story. A part of the story of this universe. Your conscious participation will be etched on the universe and on life itself. Until this universe collapses in on itself, ready to begin again. The memory of what you accomplished in your time will be the foundation for the new universe and all the life in it.